DIGITAL TOOLS FOR TEACHING

30 E-TOOLS FOR COLLABORATING, CREATING, AND PUBLISHING ACROSS THE CURRICULUM

Steve Johnson

Digital Tools for Teaching: 30 E-tools for Collaborating, Creating, and Publishing across the Curriculum

Cover Design: Studio Montage
Book layout and design: Holly Marie Gibbs
Editor: Marilee Griffin

Library of Congress Cataloging-in-Publication Data

Johnson, Steve, 1976-
 Digital tools for teaching : 30 e-tools for collaborating, creating,
and publishing across the curriculum / Steve Johnson.
       p. cm.
 Includes bibliographical references.
 ISBN 978-1-934338-84-1
1. Computer-assisted instruction. 2. Internet in education. 3.
Education--Effect of technological innovations on. I. Title.

LB1028.5.J5814 2011
371.33'44678--dc22

                   2010037430

Maupin House publishes professional resources for K-12 educators. Contact us for tailored, in-school training or to schedule an author for a workshop or conference. Visit www.maupinhouse.com for free lesson plan downloads.

Maupin House Publishing, Inc.
2416 N.W. 71st Place
Gainesville, FL 32653

www.maupinhouse.com

800-524-0634
352-373-5588
352-373-5546 (fax)
info@maupinhouse.com

10 9 8 7 6 5 4 3 2

DEDICATION

This book is dedicated to my beautiful and amazing wife for her support and to my not-as-beautiful-but-just-as-amazing dad for his inspiration.

ACKNOWLEDGEMENTS

I am very grateful to many people who have contributed to this book in both direct and indirect ways. The teachers I've worked closely with at Vass-Lakeview Elementary School, Washington Street School, and JN Fries Middle School have shaped my thoughts and passions about technology in the real world of classroom teaching. Thanks to all of you for being constant reminders of the realities of the classroom. There is no harder job in the education business than classroom teacher, and I'm honored to have been one and will always keep that reality in front of me.

The students I've worked with have had a direct influence on this book. This book is just another way for me to try and help students. I can't possibly name all the students who have had an impact on my life, and I don't want to throw out names without listing all of you. Regardless, thanks for all you've taught me!

To my personal learning network, I am humbled! I'm only as smart as the people I'm connected to, and I'm lucky to have found some excellent educators to link up with. From the #edchat discussions that push all of our thinking and urge us to action, to the random resources that have woven their way throughout this book, I'm very fortunate to have you by my side. Thanks for being my Tweeps.

To the technology facilitators and staff of Cabarrus County, North Carolina–you guys rock! Thanks for giving me a job and the freedom to pursue some really interesting projects with technology.

To Carol Baldwin and Joyce Hostetter, I want to say a special thanks. It was obviously fate that directed me to your workshop on becoming a children's book writer. Even though this book is not exactly what we worked on that week, it is indeed a direct result of your help, support, and guidance.

To my wife, Bridget, thanks for all of your support and help throughout this process. There is no way this could have happened without your words, your awesomeness, your proofreading, and your office on the weekends! To my dad, I want to say thanks for always telling me to go for it and take risks, even if it took me more than thirty years to actually do it.

TABLE OF CONTENTS

APPENDIX

INTRODUCTION

A six-year-old boy named Saulo taught me everything I need to know about using tools in the classroom.

The year was 1998, and I was fresh out of college–just a month into my first year of teaching/surviving as the only male kindergarten teacher in Moore County, North Carolina. Already, I had seen and experienced things that no college prep course could have possibly prepared me for: the daily wailing of the still four-year-old girl (who wouldn't turn five for another month); the tiny boy who was deathly afraid of the toilet; the brown-haired angel who had seemingly attached herself to my leg. I had seen, smelled, and cleaned up nearly every possible fluid that could be produced by the human body, but I still loved every minute of my work.

Saulo came to me in mid-September as the latest addition to my ever-growing class (I started the year with eighteen and ended with twenty-four). His family had just arrived in our area from Mexico, where Saulo and his five-year-old brother Servando had never been through formal schooling of any sort. The decision was made to put both boys into separate kindergarten classes. Servando (the lucky one) headed off to the wonderfully talented and experienced Mrs. Pratt. Saulo ended up with the rookie first-year teacher across the way–me.

The boys had never been apart from each other, knew absolutely no English, and had just started school for the first time. They were completely heartbroken. They screamed, they wailed, and they moaned. These tight-knit boys could hardly stand being apart, so Mrs. Pratt and I decided to try to alleviate some of their worry by setting up bean bag chairs in the windows next to our doors. Each day, these boys sat on these chairs and cried longingly at each other through the glass, across the breezeway that separated them.

With each passing day, Saulo became more and more a part of our class. Little by little, the crying slowed, and this little boy eased his way a bit more into our environment. I'd take toys and books over to his beanbag chair and even started moving the chair away from the door little by little in an attempt to bring him into the fold. After three weeks of this, Saulo was finally ready to join us. The smiles and kind words of his classmates helped lure him in (and the snacks didn't hurt, either).

I could tell right away that Saulo was bright. His big, round eyes told the story. He was one of those kids who hang on every syllable, where you can almost see their brains working as they manipulate objects. Unfortunately, in my classroom, we didn't have many objects to manipulate! When I arrived as a late hire in July (school started August 9th), the room I walked into had been vacant and subsequently used for various summer camps and programs.

In other words, it was trashed and ransacked. There were no books, no paper or pencils, and there were almost no manipulatives at all—just sixteen Unifix® cubes that I still carry with me today as a reminder of that first year.

Saulo, his classmates, and I made the best of what we had. One thing we did have was a sand table: an old, splintery wooden box on four legs so my students could stand and play with the sand inside. This was where Saulo and I really started hitting it off. He loved to dig his hands into the sand, feeling the grains slide through his fingers.

I started spending part of every school day with Saulo at the sand table. It was here that he first started to learn English. I would dig my hands into the sand and say, "sand," then he would dig his hands in and repeat the word. I'd grab a cup, and we'd practice the word "pour." I'd throw some onto his arm, make a face and say, "scratchy" and, "arm," then, "wipe it off!" He mimicked everything and, once again, his eyes told me he was getting it, one word after another. The kid was a sponge, plain and simple.

The other kids started noticing that we were spending a lot of time at this sand table and began joining the fun. They picked right up on the game and started leading the way, thinking of different ways to teach Saulo new words. Loving this new interaction with classmates, I would step back and watch in amazement. The kids truly took over; Saulo absorbed it all and, by the end of the year, was my very best reader at decoding words (the comprehension came later).

Saulo went on from there to have a very successful elementary-school career, eventually making a perfect score on his fifth grade end-of-course math exam and being highly respected by all his classmates as an extremely bright, articulate, kind soul.

Now, I want to be perfectly clear here: I had no idea what I was doing! I was just a guy trying to survive and make the best of the situation at hand. I had no training in working with Spanish-speaking students. I had no idea how to incorporate tools or utilize them correctly. I truly was a big doofus who was simply blessed with a ton of patience and a love for children.

I had no way of knowing this at the time, but that experience with Saulo completely shaped who I was to become as an educator. It taught me everything I needed to know about tools and how they are to be used in the classroom. You see, sand can be a learning tool. So can a cup. Or a smile. Everything on the planet has educational value; it just takes imagination to discover it.

It's not the tool you use with a student that makes the difference: it's what you *do* with the tool. It's what you *accomplish*. It's the *learning* that it triggers. Sand is just sand. A cup is simply a cup. A book is just paper. These things are *nothing* without the guidance, support, and imagination of a teacher.

The younger me unwittingly did some things right with Saulo. First, I identified a tool that already engaged him: the sand table. The sand and its texture fascinated Saulo. Next, I connected the tool to his primary learning need–English vocabulary. Finally, I turned the process over to my other students as they became interested, and let them lead the way while I became backup support. This allowed even more learning opportunities for Saulo and gave his classmates a sense of leadership and empowerment.

This is not rocket science. It's what we do as educators every day. We take a tool and mold it into a vehicle for delivering a relevant, engaging learning experience.

THE DIGITAL SHIFT

The tools we have at our disposal in today's classroom are changing. The old chalk blackboard is now interactive. Pens give way to computers. Publishing is becoming something done online. If you haven't already seen an influx of technology into your school and classroom, then get ready because it's coming your way! Schools reflect society, and there is no turning back from the digital age.

Right now, students are already heavily engaged with digital tools outside of classroom walls. They use these types of tools every day in meaningful ways. Like the sand that engaged Saulo, digital tools can be the connection between your students and their learning needs. Ignoring a tool that could be the key to unlocking a child's potential should not be an option. Embracing these new e-tools with your students can open up a wealth of learning opportunities that may otherwise go untapped.

For too long, we as educators have looked at e-tools as an end rather than as a means. That's because we're fascinated by the tools themselves. We're amazed that we can write with our finger on an interactive whiteboard, astounded that we can videoconference with someone halfway across the world, and in awe of the idea that we can connect with the Internet via a tiny computer that fits in the palm of our hand. Technology can often seem incredible.

For our students, however, technology is not magic. The Internet is not magic. It just is. They look at technology in a whole new way–not "How does it work?" but rather, "What can it do for me?" Google Earth is not a collection of amazing satellite images, but just a way to virtually map a route to a friend's house. Videoconferencing is not an astounding means of communication in real time with people across the world; it's a means to understanding another person's culture. This is a powerful shift that I urge you to similarly adopt as you teach by moving away from the "how/why" of technology and more towards the "what."As in, what can these technology tools *do* for my students?

If you're like most teachers, you understand that digital tools are here with us from now on, and you are quite aware that these tools are increasingly central to the lives of your students. You just may not have enjoyed the support you needed to learn to use them effectively; that is, just like any other tool you use for teaching. If your district or school is like many I have seen, the emphasis has been placed on buying equipment, not on training teachers how to use it well.

Undoubtedly, you've heard the phrases "twenty-first century skills," or "twenty-first century classrooms," and have been expected to become a "twenty-first century teacher"–all with no clear definition as to what these terms exactly mean. Through this book, I hope to show you that these terms can be defined around three main concepts: allowing your students to collaborate both locally and globally, creating products using e-tools, and publishing students' creations to the Internet for enjoyment, assessment, and the development of their digital footprints.

USING E-TOOLS FOR LEARNING

This book aims to give you the support you need to begin to use e-tools in the same way that you use other, more familiar classroom tools: for learning.

The e-tools chosen for this book will get you started on the path of incorporating digital tools into your classroom effectively, *but this book is not about tools*. It's about learning. It's about changing your teaching perspective so that you connect digital tools with the content you want to teach. You will be connecting your teaching to the e-tools that your students find relevant to their lives. You will be creating an engaging learning experience using e-tools, in the same way that you create engaging lessons without them.

Consider the thirty technology tools described in this book simply as cups and sand. The projects list the tools and suggest ways to incorporate them into your curricula to meet the learning needs of your students. As always, it's up to you to provide the courage, imagination, and determination needed to make an impact. The world is changing, your classroom is changing, your students are changing, and this book looks to help you meet these changes head on.

WHAT IS IN THIS BOOK

The first four chapters define the characteristics of today's students, some of the core skills they will need to succeed in a digital future, how to get started using e-tools in your classroom, and how to assess the digital products your students will start creating.

After that, thirty alphabetical e-tools that you can use in any content area are described in detail. Each tool contains a goal, summary, what you'll need to get started, as well as several ideas for using it in each core content area: language arts, math, science, and social studies.

Accompanying this book is a new resource to help teachers on their path to success-fully implementing these e-tools in the classroom: my website, **www.edtechsteve.com**. There, you will find short videos for each tool that show in plain language how to use and incorporate these new tools in your classroom. Also included within this site are forms for you to request new tool videos, suggest more ideas, and send any corrections or updates you think are important. The point of this site is for it to be a living, breathing resource for all teachers. Please hop on there and become part of the expanding com-munity of teachers using e-tools successfully with students!

In the Appendix, you will find a list of some more great tools that simply didn't "make the cut" for one reason or another. Following this, I link all of the tools to the International Society for Technology in Education (ISTE)'s standards for students. Finally, there is a list of real-life case studies that show how teachers actually applied different e-tools into their classrooms.

You probably won't want to read these tool descriptions one after another. Don't worry—they are designed to be picked through and bookmarked. The following chart provides tool names, page numbers, and goals sorted in three general categories: e-tools for newbies, developing users, and advanced users. Use these charts to guide your reading and help you choose the tool's capabilities and comfort level that suits you.

NOTE If a technical word or phrase stumps you while reading, check the "Glossary of Digital Terms" in the Appendix.

TOOLS FOR NEWBIES

TOOL NAME	PAGE	GOAL
Animoto	40	Produce a professional-looking video with pictures and music
Blogs	42	Create an online journal that conveys thoughts, feelings, and constructs knowledge
Digital Storytelling	46	Tells a story with images, text, and music
Glogster	50	Create and share an online multimedia poster that can include text, graphics, images, video, and audio
Google Earth	54	Explore the Earth, Moon, and Mars through high-quality satellite imagery
Image Editing and Enhancement	58	Edit and enhance digital photos in creative and fun ways
Message Boards	62	Provide an online space for discussion through text
Timeline Creators	82	Create an interactive timeline that can be published
TodaysMeet	84	Create an easy, accessible chat room
Wikis	94	Collaborate on activities with an easy-to-edit website
Word Clouds	96	Analyze word use through creation of a picture

TOOLS FOR DEVELOPING USERS

TOOL NAME	PAGE	GOAL
Collaborative Whiteboards	44	Share online whiteboard space for collaborative activities
ePals	48	Connect with, and learn from, students and teachers around the world
Google Docs	52	Collaboratively create and edit presentations, spreadsheets, and word processing documents
Google Forms	56	Create surveys or tests that are automatically inserted into a spreadsheet for easy data collection and analysis
Mind Mapping	64	Create interactive graphic organizers by students, independently or through collaboration
Podcasting	68	Record and produce an audio recording
Screen Recording	74	Create instructional videos by screen capturing the actions on your computer screen
SlideShare	78	Upload, share, and research presentations
Video Conferencing	88	Connect with others via live video streamed over the Internet
VoiceThread	90	Engage in a group conversation around pictures, documents, and video
Website Creators	92	Create easily published interactive websites
Zoho	98	Utilize a wide array of online tools to create, share and collaborate

TOOLS FOR ADVANCED USERS

TOOL NAME	PAGE	GOAL
Live Internet Video Streaming	60	Stream live video over the Internet that is open to the public to view
Ning	66	Create a safe social networking site for students and teachers to communicate and interact
Prezi	70	Create a visually distinctive, interactive presentation
SchoolTube	72	Access an online space to view and publish safe, moderated videos originating with students worldwide
Second Life	76	Provide a virtual world where users can interact with objects, settings, and other users in real time
Spore Creature Creator	80	Create interesting creatures that activate student thinking
Twitter	86	Establish connections and communication to a wide audience

Read on, have fun, and make sure to connect with me via **www.edtechsteve.com** to let me know your thoughts and ideas for integrating technology into the classroom!

DISCLAIMER:

Neither Maupin House Publishing, Inc. nor I have any affiliation whatsoever with the websites or digital tools mentioned in this book. Each digital tool and/or website may have its own terms of use, privacy, or copyright policies that should be complied with.

Teachers should always check with their school system's specific rules and policies in regards to the use of technology with students. This includes parental permissions, student use of equipment, and publication of student likenesses or work.

Always keep current copyright law in mind when publishing products online, especially when dealing with the music, art, videos, etc., of others. The US Copyright Office (www.copyright.gov) is an excellent resource to familiarize teachers and students with copyright law.

When students are utilizing the Internet, take all precautions necessary to protect them under your care. Be sure to run through any Internet-based project or research before allowing students the opportunity to access related websites.

All tools and tool descriptions were correct as of the writing of this book. Updates to tools as they evolve will be posted to my website, **www.edtechsteve.com**. Feel free to submit updates or corrections there as well.

PART I

USING DIGITAL TOOLS IN THE CLASSROOM

CHAPTER ONE:
UNDERSTANDING TODAY'S TECH-SAVVY LEARNER

Let's begin where all aspects of education should naturally start: the learner. It is critically important to come to know the learners at each and every level of educational theory and practice. The better you know your "customers," the better you can serve them.

In school settings, generational and cultural gaps can create a disconnect from the very top on down, from policy makers at the federal or state level to classroom teachers who are expected to faithfully execute these policies on a day-to-day basis. Become more familiar with today's students and you become more in tune with their needs and how you can meet them. At every level of education, knowing how this generation of students views and experiences the world can lead to powerful, positive change.

Of course, it's a bit dangerous to assign characteristics that define a generation. Not everyone fits neatly in a category, and everyone adds his or her own unique personality to the broader age group of which they are a part. Some students still like to read books (on paper, even!) instead of texting their friends, or prefer attending traditional lectures instead of interacting with peers. There are certainly many students who, because of conditions of poverty, have hardly had the chance to connect to the Internet at all. However, despite these exceptions, it is helpful to take a look at the broader character-istics that this generation displays so that we may get a better idea of what most of our students want and need in the digital age.

First, understand that your students are growing up with something no other generation before them has ever experienced: virtually unlimited information at their fingertips. In *The World is Flat: A Brief History of the Twenty-first Century*, author Thomas L. Friedman says this unique access is one of the major "flatteners" of our world today. He quotes the chairman and CEO of Google, Inc., Eric Schmidt:

Search is so highly personal that searching is empowering for humans like nothing else. It is the antithesis of being taught. It is about self-empowerment; it is empowering indi-viduals to do what they think best with the information they want. It is very different from anything else that preceded it. Radio was one-to-many. TV was one-to-many. The tele-phone was one-to-one. Search is the ultimate expression of the power of the individual, using a computer, looking at the world, and finding exactly what they want–and everyone is different when it comes to that. (P. 183)

This sends a powerful (and somewhat nerve-wracking) message to educators: outside of school, our students are experiencing a highly customized, personal world. They have information at their fingertips. Our job title can no longer be "Master Distributor of

> Our job title can no longer be "Master Distributor of Information."

Information." Teachers who are still holding onto the idea that they are the gatekeepers of knowledge are the new dinosaurs. Google has killed them off, whether they know it or not.

Going forward, our jobs must be about giving our students personalized, relevant instruction that develops their ability to make *meaningful sense* of the information-rich world they live in. Sure, they can find anything and everything under the sun on the Internet—but do they know what to do with it? Can they evaluate the accuracy of what they read? Can they analyze and organize this glut of information? How does it improve their lives? *They* may have the world at their fingertips, but *we* have the power to guide them towards molding it into something worth creating.

What else can we learn about this generation to better serve them, given the realities of the digital world we are living in? Don Tapscott, author of *Growing Up Digital: The Rise of the Net Generation* (1997) and co-author of *Wikinomics: How Mass Collaboration Changes Everything* (2006) is a widely hailed authority on this topic. His latest work, *Grown Up Digital: How the Net Generation is Changing Your World* (2009) tells the story of the results of a $4 million research project that included input from over six thousand members of the Net Generation — a term coined by Mr. Tapscott to describe those born between January 1977 and December 1997.

"As the first global generation ever, the Net Geners are smarter, quicker, and more tolerant of diversity than their predecessors." — Don Tapscott in *Grown Up Digital: How the Net Generation is Changing Your World*

The data shows that the Net Generation shares eight characteristics. As **collaborators,** they would much rather engage in a conversation than listen to a lecture. Because they are **scrutinizers,** they have the ability to pick apart and fact-check information they are presented with. As **fun seekers,** Net Geners pursue entertainment in all aspects of their world; as **integrity hounds,** they expect that world to be truthful and transparent. As **speed chasers,** they have grown accustomed to getting what they want or need quickly. As **innovation hunters,** they place value on what innovative technology can *do* for them, and as **freedom finders** they place a premium on having choices. And, finally, as **customizers** they want to express their individuality through everything they come in contact with, whether it is the wallpaper of their computer, the skin of their iPod, or the avatar that represents them in their video games. (Tapscott, pp. 73-96)

Identifying and accommodating these generational needs can have powerful, positive effects in your classroom. Let's explore how.

COLLABORATORS

Those of us who have taught for a decade or so have probably noticed that our classes are starting to talk more than they want to listen. It is simply more natural for this generation of students to engage in a conversation than to sit and listen to a lecture. This group of students has interacted with their environment in fundamentally different ways from any previous generation.

Outside of school, they are no longer passive recipients of content. Instead, they are able to interact with information through the Internet, chat via social networking tools about what they like or dislike, and find others like themselves to analyze and discuss their favorite shows, actors, musicians, and anything else they enjoy. The world they are growing up in is one in which problems will be solved through an online community, rather than an individual hammering away by themselves.

As they grow older, they'll bounce ideas off one another from anywhere in the world in real time. There can be no doubt that this is the direction the world is moving, with the widespread development of social networking sites such as Twitter, and collaborative, document-building tools like Google Docs. This highly collaborative environment will shape the world in the years to come.

What this means for your classroom: Your students are natural socializers who would rather work together than alone. They are more likely to learn if they are engaging both their teacher and their peers—for example, if they are able to ask questions, give and receive ideas, and in general, talk about the content being presented. To accommodate this, your classroom might need to be a little noisy! Students should be talking about the concept at hand and working together to better understand content.

New e-tools that facilitate collaboration take advantage of this characteristic. Wikis, blogs, social networking, Google Docs, chat rooms, message boards, and a host of other online tools outlined in this book give your students the ability to collaborate online with their classmates and with peers from around the globe.

SCRUTINIZERS

Have you been fact-checked by a student yet? Have you presented information to students who then go to the Internet to verify or attempt to discredit what you're saying? Perhaps you have, or perhaps your students have just been polite and not told you what they've been doing! Either way, the world these students have grown up in has allowed them ample opportunity to check up on any and everything they are shown or told. The information is out there and they will find it if given motivation (and what better motivation than to prove their teacher wrong?).

These kids have also grown up in the age of Adobe Photoshop and airbrushing. They understand that the images they are being shown often have an inherent bias. They know that models don't always look like what the pictures illustrate, and they have grown up seeing famous people and politicians swept up in scandals that tarnish the public images they work so hard to maintain. Because of this world they've grown up in, they are natural scrutinizers of content.

What this means for your classroom: The first thing is that you're going to have to get over the annoyance factor of this characteristic! One of my personal pet peeves as a teacher has always been when students try to correct me (especially when they're right!) Instead of getting frustrated, actively encourage your students to probe and question the material they are working with.

Deeper understanding emerges from deeper questioning. When a student confidently tells you, "I read on the Internet that the reason Pluto isn't considered a planet anymore is because of a conspiracy among the scientific community," don't shut that conversation off. Instead, dive into it. Have students dig up the source of their information and share it with the class for discussion. If the information is true, you've taught your students a lesson in dealing with a changing information landscape. If the information is false, your students have experienced a lesson in how to analyze Internet sources. Either way, you have shown them something important and modeled a process that is critically important to their future learning in a digital environment.

Finally, shifting your mindset away from seeing yourself as the sole "expert" in the class-room is probably the most important thing you can do to address your students' need to scrutinize. Instead, think of sharing the investigative journey with your students. This is not easy at first, but the more you practice it, the easier (and less annoying) it becomes!

FUN SEEKERS

Tapscott's research revealed that the Net Generation has a widespread expectation of work being *fun*. They view their possible career paths not merely as making X amounts of money or gaining certain levels of security. Rather, they think in terms of whether or not their jobs will be fun and will bring them happiness.

This is a large shift from how previous generations viewed the concept of work–as an endeavor completely separate from the rest of their lives. Fun took a backseat to provid-ing for the family, which has traditionally been the driving force for previous generations.

Today, this has changed. In fact, to land the best and the brightest, many companies are now going to great lengths to make the work environment a fun place to be. Google is leading the way in this shift, providing their workers time for recreation and time to pursue their own personal goals, while still "on the clock." With the success that Google has had with this model, many major corporations are moving in this direction as well.

What this means for your classroom: Your students expect fun at school as well. The simplest way to incorporate this need into your classroom is to let your hair down and have some fun! There is nothing in the teacher manual that says your job can't be interesting and happy for both you and your students.

I've heard many teachers preach the old mantra of "Don't smile before Christmas." My fear is that, with this generation, if *you* don't smile before Christmas, *they* might not smile until June, when they finally get to leave. Laugh with your students, connect with them, let them express their own creativity, and maintain a welcoming environment. You might be surprised to see how this influences the work they produce for you.

INTEGRITY HOUNDS

The Net Generation places a high value on the integrity of the person, government, or company they are dealing with. They expect people or institutions to be truthful, straightforward, fair, and transparent. These fact-checkers don't like it when they feel they've been misled. Openness and transparency are huge issues that have a large effect on society, and this generation demands it. They want the rationale behind decisions that are being made ("Because I said so" drives them crazy). They want to see the inner workings and decide for themselves if it passes their integrity test.

The Net Generation has grown up in a world of widely reported personal, political, and corporate scandals, producing a level of openness never before attained (and which will only grow with the spread of social networking). In today's world, anyone with a cell phone is a real-time reporter to a community of millions. Without cell phones and social networking sites such as Twitter, how much would the world have known about the disputed Iranian presidential elections in the summer of 2009? The world truly is becoming a tougher and tougher place to hide.

What this means for your classroom: Your students will want to know exactly where they stand with you. To incorporate this need for transparency in your classroom, start with the grading process. Students should know exactly on what criteria their grades are based. Show them work samples that receive varying grades and talk through the process that produces the samples' grades.

Extend this idea to your students' parents as well; make sure that all projects, quizzes, or tests are laid out in full for all to see. Post this information on your class website, blog, wiki, or social networking service and encourage parents to read and comment.

If there is a subjective aspect to your grading process, lay out that process for all of your students and parents to see. Model your thought processes, and encourage any of them to ask questions *before* you give the first assignment, project, test, or quiz. The more transparent your classroom becomes, the better equipped your students will be to meet your expectations.

SPEED CHASERS

As digital access becomes faster and more accessible, this Net Gen characteristic is beginning to span multiple generations. For the Net Generation especially, the need for speed is enormous. They expect fast results. They want to ask a question and have it answered immediately. This can sometimes detract students from developing deeper meaning from content-related activities. They always seem to be jumping ahead and forming conclusions based on little evidence.

It's very possible that this behavior stems from the instant gratification of the Internet and how kids have come to rely on it to give quick answers. Having grown up in a world of high-speed Internet and exponentially faster computing devices, the Net Geners have not experienced the same growing pains with sluggish technology that the rest of us grew up with. Communication to them is in real time. They rarely e-mail anymore—it's too slow! With the rise of Internet-capable mobile devices that can connect in more and more places, the speed with which they can communicate and research information has increased considerably and will continue to do so for the foreseeable future.

What this means for your classroom: Sometimes, the issue of digital speed is out of your hands. Technology-wise, your IT department most likely controls the model of computer your students are using as well, as the speed of your Internet connection. There's not much you can do about this unless you actively involve yourself in the purchasing process at your school.

In a more general sense, you can help your students by creating an environment where careful reflection is a cornerstone for success. Modeling this process yourself is key. When reading a novel, instead of simply asking the students "What do you think will happen next?" you should model the process of going back and thinking about the previous text and any hints it may provide.

This modeling process can also be very important when interacting with technology. I've seen many teachers get frustrated in front of their students when technology is not working fast enough, then turn around and point fingers when the students start to express this same frustration! Building an environment where technology issues are part of the problem-solving process will go a long way towards easing your students' need for speed in the classroom.

Beyond the speed of the technology you're using, this characteristic also manifests itself in the classroom through the feedback your students are expecting. Feedback to this generation is often instantaneous: when they search something, they get quick results. When they play a game, they know instantly where they stand and what else they need to accomplish their goals. Your students expect classroom feedback to operate in much the same way, and will crave a speedy response to the work they are doing. Because of this characteristic, it is more important than ever to provide prompt feedback on assignments, tests, and projects.

INNOVATION HUNTERS

Something new and cool is always coming out in the world today. Technology tools are ever-changing, and they offer us more and more options to view and shape our world. Your students have lived in this ever-evolving world of high-tech tools since the day they were born. New technology is not a big deal to them. (Keep reminding yourself: to your students, *technology is not magic*. The Internet is not magic. It just *is*.)

For example, the TV in my living room has fingerprints all over it. Why? Because my three-year-old has been playing with my iPod touch and now thinks everything is a touch screen! Older generations look at a piece of new technology and say "Wow!" The Net Generation looks at a piece of new technology and says, "What does it *do*?" Students are interested in new technology, not because it's cool, but because of what it can accomplish for them.

What this means for your classroom: To fully take advantage of this characteristic for learning, you're going to have to turn over control of tools to your students. Don't tell your students what a new piece of technology or e-tool does. Hand it over to them, let them figure it out, then *let them tell you and the rest of the class what it does.*

A perfect example of this is the growing number of interactive whiteboards showing up in classrooms across the world (you might even have one in your classroom). In so many classrooms, all this new piece of technology does is the same thing the old whiteboard did: serve as a place to project presentations or have the teacher write notes for students to dutifully copy. What a waste of money and innovation!

Instead, I encourage you to turn new technology over to the students and let them explore the possibilities. Then have them explain what types of things it has to offer for helping them learn your content. You might be surprised at what you find out. These innovation hunters are well versed in collaborating and figuring out the ins and outs of technology, so use this to your advantage in the classroom as much as possible. Encourage your students to investigate new trends in technology that allow them a greater potential to change the world.

FREEDOM FINDERS

Without a doubt, this generation of kids has enjoyed greater freedoms and choices than any previous generation. Think about it: from hundreds of channels to watch on TV, to a myriad of clubs and activities in and outside of school, to hundreds of video games and video game systems, to millions of Internet destinations, to all of the different styles of clothing to express themselves with, to a huge assortment of reading material (and ways in which to read it), it's easy to see how today's society puts a premium on freedom and choice. Students today are immersed in this world and crave the chance to make meaningful choices in all areas of their lives. It is a part of who they are.

Now, contrast the immersion in choices that students experience *outside* of school with what happens *inside* the traditional school. How many choices are students making? Are they making meaningful decisions that impact how they learn? Increasing their choices is a worthy challenge for you to undertake.

One way to meet this challenge is by giving students choices as to which products they create in your classroom. Within the products they create, don't prescribe what the output needs to look like to be correct as long as the content is covered (content is *always* king).

Another way to increase the sense of freedom of choice: Give students a voice in the management of the class, and respect their opinions as class rules and procedures are created. Allow students to give suggestions about how they will be assessed. As teachers, we're always complaining that we get handed down programs or new curricula and not given any say in how it was decided. Well, this is exactly how most students feel! Recognizing the need for increased choice is an all-important first step.

With more choice and more freedom in the classroom, keep in mind that you are setting your students up to make more mistakes. *This is great!* Allowing the freedom to make mistakes simply opens up more powerful learning opportunities for you and your students. Create and maintain a classroom environment that places value on gaining knowledge through failure.

CUSTOMIZERS

Tapscott represents customization as a Net Gen desire to personalize products and experiences. Net Geners want to change the ringtones on their phones, alter the wall-paper on their computers, record live TV to watch at their convenience, create their own unique online presence, and often spend as much time changing the look of their video game character as they actually spend playing the game! Simply put, our students want to express their individuality through their appearance, accessories, and the products they create.

What this means for your classroom: By allowing students to express themselves through the products they create, we are accommodating the need for customization. If they are creating a slideshow, why not allow them to bring in their own background music? If they are creating a digital story, why not allow them to use images they feel are appropriate?

This represents yet another shift in control from teacher to student. While addressing this characteristic seems like a small shift, it can nonetheless provide interesting insight into your students that can help you connect on a personal level. On a deeper level, when your students customize their products, they are telling you something important about who they are and what they value.

Putting content first holds the key to placing customization in a learning context. Let students know that they are not allowed to personalize or customize until they have learned and represented the content they are responsible for. If creating a biographical slide-show about Thomas Jefferson, for example, the slides should be filled with information about his life, his vision of government, and his ideas about our nation *before* any music, backgrounds, or animations are added.

The customized choices your students make should always be linked to the content represented. Force students to justify the customization choices they have made within their work ("Why did you choose Kid Rock to represent Custer's Last Stand?"). If they cannot reasonably reconcile the choices they've made with the content they are working on, then the choices need to be revisited and reworked.

So, these are our students. What kinds of skills do we need to teach them so they can be successful?

CHAPTER TWO:
PREPARING STUDENTS
FOR THEIR DIGITAL FUTURE

In 2006, noted thinker Karl Fisch said, "We are currently preparing students for jobs that don't yet exist, using technologies that haven't been invented, in order to solve problems we don't even know are problems yet."

Every generation of teachers could justifiably say that preparing students for an unknown future full of changes has always been a challenge. However, perhaps because of the effects of a rapidly changing technology, the world seems to be changing faster, too.

We are overwhelmed with information coming at us from everywhere. How do we prepare students to read and evaluate this information? How do we prepare them to be fully fluent in a digital age? What are the important skills they will need to master in a future defined by digital tools?

> Students today need to be able to create meaningful products with digital tools.

Let's take a look at Bloom's Taxonomy of Educational Objectives to give us some insights about how to answer these questions. Since its original publication in 1956, Bloom's Taxonomy has laid the foundation for a large portion of how instruction is designed and developed across the world. In 2001, two former colleagues of Benjamin Bloom collaborated to publish a newly revised version of the original taxonomy. The two men responsible for the revision, Lorin Anderson and David Krathwohl, methodically reworked the taxonomy over a six-year period, from 1995-2001.

The result of their work, titled *A Taxonomy for Learning, Teaching, and Assessing: A Revision of Bloom's Taxonomy of Educational Objectives* (2001), successfully updated Bloom's taxonomy for the twenty-first century. Their revision serves as a powerful reminder of the critical importance we should place on actively engaging our students in the creation process.

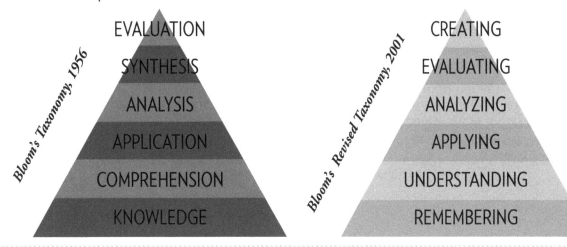

Apart from changing the wording of the taxonomy from nouns to verbs, the most obvious change in structure is seen at the very top. Creating is now understood to be the pinnacle of learning outcomes within the taxonomy. Today's learners must be able to manipulate e-tools to create meaningful products for a variety of audiences.

The products they create with e-tools will demonstrate that they have mastered the content you have taught them. Creating a product incorporates several important higher-order skills: students are problem solving, making justified choices, and managing their time in order to finish a task.

This process of creating a product also incorporates nicely with the characteristics of this generation of students. It offers opportunities for students to customize the product they are building so they can showcase their individual nature and creativity. It is more fun to create a product than to sit and listen to a lecture.

Our students will increasingly need to rely on the skill of creation when they enter college or the workforce. In the near future, admission into college and finding a quality job will more likely be about the types of things you can create online and less about an SAT score or grade-point average. The process of selecting a product to create offers the choices and freedom this generation craves.

The amount of choices and the instructional power of each is staggering. Digital tools make it easier than ever for our students to express their creativity while showing what they know. Videos can be recorded and uploaded; stories can be digitally told using images and composed or selected music; timelines can become interactive; avatars can be customized to fit learning objectives; screen recordings can demonstrate learning; multimedia-based posters can be easily produced, and on and on.

Students will need to be able to collaborate. Our students are already living in a world where successful collaboration is an increasingly critical skill to master. Just two examples tell the story of where we are now: the move to cloud computing, where documents and operating systems are housed, managed, and worked on together by people in different physical locations; and social networking, a worldwide phenomenon that connects people and allows them to share important information, photographs, and videos, thus influencing virtually every aspect of our culture.

The best way to get started with collaboration is by having students engage in the content you are teaching through some of the collaborative technology tools in this book. Blogs, wikis, or message boards are a good place to start. Setting up a social networking site such as a Ning would bring your students into an interactive learning environment that is similar to sites they're familiar with, like Facebook and MySpace. There are many opportunities to collaborate in producing a product, such as a Google Doc, mind map, timeline, website, or digital story. There are tools to aid in real-time collaboration, such as chat rooms, online whiteboard conferencing, or Web conferencing. Tools like ePals, video conferencing, and Twitter take the idea of collaboration to a worldwide stage.

Students will need to communicate well with e-tools. Teachers of past generations taught students how to read, write, and speak effectively. To that list, today's teachers must add the skill of digital fluency: the ability to communicate well on the Internet. This means publishing their work online, which creates a very important digital footprint, the products they leave behind on the Internet.

Our digital footprint tells people who we are, what we have been working on, who we are working with, and what we have accomplished. Far too many students don't pay attention to the products they leave behind on the Internet–nor do they realize that this record will follow them long past school. Yet, a digital footprint— the trail of postings and products that we leave behind when we access the Internet—can make or break a student's future.

In June 2009, a Harris Interactive Poll found that 45 percent of surveyed employers admitted to using social networking site to screen job candidates, up from 22 percent just the year before. Eleven percent of employers who had not previously used social networking to screen applicants stated that they would start doing so in 2010. What this means is that by the time our students enter the workforce or apply to college, their digital footprint will likely be the first impression they give to a prospective school or employer.

The good news is that the study clearly showed that employers not only use digital footprints to *disregard* candidates, but they also use them to help *hire* the right individuals. This provides an enormous opportunity for us as educators.

Plainly put, it is quickly becoming our duty to make sure that we not only share this information with our students, but also actively guide them toward creating a positive digital footprint that will carry with them throughout their careers and lives. By publishing their work, we have the chance to help our students build a powerful online presence that can showcase their skills, creativity, and personality.

Ideally, everything that your students create in your classroom should be published in some form or another. Whether it is an Animoto video, a Glog from Glogster, a story through VoiceThread, or any of the other tools laid out in this book, the more your students publish, the better.

Even if you have students create something with traditional tools, like paper, shoeboxes, sticky notes etc., you can still publish this work to the Internet through websites, blogs, images, wikis, message boards, and so on. When your students leave your class at the end of the year, they should be able to hop onto a computer and share this portfolio with their parents.

Publication also encourages students to create their products with an audience in mind. The choices they make are affected by those that will see it. You will also find that when students are publishing their work for their parents, peers, and anyone else to see, they will be more likely to put forth the effort to make it a high-quality piece.

There is also a possibility that the products your students create could attract a larger audience than you or they could imagine! Take the case of Gregg Breinberg, a chorus teacher in New York City's P.S. 22, as a prime example. In the summer of 2006, he started a YouTube channel and blog that featured his chorus students singing contemporary songs. According to the P.S. 22 blog (**www.ps22chorus.blogspot.com**), these videos have had over 21 million views to date! At this time of this writing, the channel has recorded more than fourteen hundred positive comments left for these students. The chorus has performed for famous musicians and politicians, and has taken the stage in front of thousands of fans. These students' lives have been fundamentally changed by a teacher taking the time to publish and showcase his students' hard work.

E-TOOLS GET STUDENTS READY FOR THEIR FUTURE

So how do we get students ready for a highly collaborative, technology-driven environment? By providing this type of environment throughout their schooling, of course. The good news is that your students are ready to begin this process, as they've most likely already participated in online collaboration in one form or another. Their generation's need to collaborate will pay big dividends when you start incorporating this skill into your classroom.

Once you've begun using e-tools, you'll see your work bear fruit immediately. Your students will become more engaged with the content at hand, because it is delivered in a more meaningful, connected way. Opening up the conversation will allow ideas to be more fully developed by the group. You will start to notice your typically quiet students becoming more engaged when given the opportunity to express their thoughts online.

You may be surprised to see that your students already have the ability to take a topic and flesh it out from multiple directions while functioning online. They will, of course, need guidance and structure to keep focused on content, but the results from emphasizing this skill with students will be immediately apparent.

You don't need thirty laptops, an interactive whiteboard, a document camera, integrated speakers, a classroom quiz system, and MP3 players for each student to make this vision a reality. For most of the tools listed in this book, all you need to get started is one computer and possibly a projector to showcase student work.

I understand that many of the activities you'll want to do with students may require access to a computer lab that is overbooked and/or not well-maintained. The simple reality within many schools is that the amount of technology present does not allow for effective daily use. But there is one more reality I'll share with you: if you don't have it now, it's coming. The shift to put technology into the hands of students is well underway and is gaining steam each year. In fact, many districts are moving toward a one-to-one model, where every student has a computer or computing device. Ignoring digital tools is no longer going to be an option. Embracing it now puts you ahead of the curve and your students on a more successful path.

Creating a learning environment that incorporates e-tools means your excellent teaching strategies are placed in an engaging context that your learners find relevant. For example, let's say you are doing a unit on the different types of rocks. In the past, you may have started with some knowledge-building through books or encyclopedias, where students could see the different types of rocks through pictures. You might have then taken them outside to find and categorize rocks on their own. They might have written letters to geologists or people from other regions to ask questions or compare types of rocks in different locales. From there, they may have built a diorama, poster, or other display to show the rocks they had found and the information they learned from studying rocks in your class. Your students might have then been asked to make a presentation to the class, relating what they learned. Their display would then go into a public place in the school—on the wall, in the media center, or in the lobby for all to see and comment on.

Let me be perfectly clear: *there is nothing wrong with these methods*. They incorporate outstanding, authentic learning strategies. However, you can easily incorporate e-tools to make these methods even more relevant and engaging for today's students. In this case, for example, some methods could include:

→ Building base knowledge through Internet research, online activities, interactive diagrams that students can draw on and manipulate, etc.

→ Going outside and letting students take digital pictures or video of what they are finding. With iPods or laptops, students record observations and provide guesses as to which type of rock they have found and why.

→ Having students interview each other about the rocks they found and why they believe they are a certain type. This can be done via podcast or through video.

→ Having students use GPS devices to mark places where certain rocks were located and make guesses as to why certain types of rocks were found in one place and not another.

→ Having students get in touch via e-mail, chat, or video conferencing with geologists for insight into why they are finding certain types of rocks around their school.

→ Having students contact another class through ePals to communicate about the similarities and differences of rocks in each area.

→ Having students create and publish a video that details their findings and what they've learned.

→ Having students blog about their thoughts and feelings about the project.

→ Having students create and publish a Glog that illustrates their understandings through multimedia.

→ Creating a Ning where students can upload files, blog, give and receive comments, and post information to manage the unit.

These are just a few ideas that could accompany this type of unit. As you can see, e-tools, used wisely, support good teaching.

CHAPTER THREE:
GETTING STARTED
USING E-TOOLS FOR LEARNING

GENERAL CLASSROOM ENVIRONMENT

Your classroom environment should attempt to incorporate as many of the generational needs identified in Chapter One as possible. And, the overarching quality your classroom needs is an atmosphere of mutual respect. Students must have respect for their teacher, their peers, and the global community with which they will be collaborating. Teachers must be willing to listen and learn, too.

Now and in the future, value will come from the community working together to discuss ideas and solve problems. The freedom to acknowledge strengths, shortcomings, and mistakes is a critical component in preparing your students for success when they leave school. Mutual respect should seep into every part of the environment you build with your students.

Implementing major changes in the classroom is not easy or smooth. There will be moments where you'll want to scrap it and dive back into what you've always done. My hope is that the needs of your students and your desire to see them through to long-lasting success will drive you forward. Hopefully, the following insights will help you through your growing pains.

Let Students Lead the Way. Most of us grew up in the "teacher as supreme knowledge holder" era. If the teacher didn't know it, the book did. Our own teaching methods often incorporate this assumption, whether or not we're consciously aware of it.

For example, I can clearly remember teaching an interactive whiteboard lesson on different types of triangles when a fifth-grader corrected me on something I was telling the class about classification. Unsure of who was right, I put the question to the side, saying, "Let's figure that one out when I'm done."

This was completely the wrong thing to do! What *should* I have done? That's easy: I should have invited the student up, given him complete control of the tools, and had him lead the way in instructing all of us in what he was thinking. The student, his peers, and I all would have benefitted from such an approach.

Control and power are not easy to relinquish. It requires a fundamental shift in mindset; one that embraces the value, depth, and knowledge of today's students who have grown up immersed in information. Quite simply, many students will know things that we don't. You've undoubtedly experienced this with your students; some of them are experts on the most seemingly random topics! It's time for us as educators to value our students by occasionally letting go of the reins and seeing where the horses want to pull us.

The easiest way to start letting your students lead is to value their input and expertise. If they feel that a test is unfair, have them design a better way to demonstrate their knowledge. If a student has issues getting his or her website to post correctly, have another student lend a hand. If a student read something online that contradicts the textbook, validate this concern and ask other students to help research the truth. As the saying goes, your students should be the ones tired at the end of the day—not you!

In regards to online tools, Don Tapscott said that we are entering a "unique period in human history where for the first time, children are an authority on something that is really important. I was an authority on model trains when I was a kid. Today, children are an authority on the big revolution that is changing every institution in society. It is already affecting schools profoundly. The kids know more than their educators about the biggest innovation in learning ever." (Gerstner, 1999).

Of course, many students do not have access to digital tools, but the point rings true for most: they are more comfortable with technology and its many uses. Kids today are more likely to dive right in and try something online. My advice to you is to let them! If new technology lands in your room, let the students unpack it. Let them help put it together.

Even better, hand it off to them, let them figure it out, and then have them teach you and the rest of the class what it does. When tackling one of the e-tools in this book for the first time, allow your students a chance to play and experiment with it, then share what they've found. Especially in the area of these digital tools, it makes sense to allow your students to lead the way.

Finally, if you want to know how to improve your classroom, I'll suggest something very scary: asking your students. Ask them how they believe they could play a larger part in day-to-day activities and projects. Ask them what types of learning activities work best. Ask them what they like or dislike about working in groups and for possible solutions to those issues. Giving more choices to students can be a very scary shift, but it can pay big dividends in today's technology-rich classroom.

Embrace Mistakes. Mistakes and learning go hand in hand. If you think back on your life, I'd wager that the most important lessons you learned emerged from a mistake or failure of some sort. Failing is a part of being human and should not be looked at negatively, but rather as an opportunity. It is in the moments of failure that our greatest and most important learning occurs. This should become your classroom mantra as you start to undertake the changes suggested in this book and start using technology tools that you are uncomfortable with.

And make no mistake: You are going to make mistakes. The e-tool that you've based a week's worth of lesson plans on will freeze up. The projector bulb will blow. You will give incorrect directions. Your students will call you out on facts. You'll put students into groups that simply don't work. You'll call on your students to help with a technology issue and it'll be something obvious ("Did you plug it in?").

These things are going to happen. Always remember that it is not the mistakes that define you, it's how you respond. Do you throw your hands in the air and give up? Do you curse the technology gods? Do you snap at your students for daring to correct you? The way that you react will be the way that they react as they encounter the same problems.

Your students are watching. They are learning more from the way that you react to failure than anything else you're trying to teach them. If you want your students to approach mistakes as learning opportunities, you have to embrace this idea yourself. To model this, make a conscious effort to invite your students into the problem-solving process.

Think aloud to illustrate your thinking. For example, let's say you have your students in the computer lab, all logged in, and you're about to show them how to get into Google Earth. But when you zoom in to a particular city, the image stays blurred because the Internet connection is inactive. Don't get worried that your lesson is ruined, because the inadvertent lesson behind the lesson is about to begin. Speak aloud about your feelings: "I just tried this yesterday and it worked fine; now I'm getting a bit peeved that when we need it most, it cuts us off."

Don't go into a panic, checking every cable while the students sit quietly, watching the drama unfold. Instead, have them attempt to log into the program and see if it's a problem for all of the computers. Work through the troubleshooting process and ask your students to give ideas as to what the issue could be. Try a few ideas out and see if they work, but if they don't, move on and try something else to deliver the content of the day. Come back later when the issue has been fixed by your technology department and carry on as normal. Don't dwell on the malfunction of the day. Instead, show your students that it's important to be flexible and move on.

This is nothing new to you, as a teacher. The traditional tools you've used before have broken and you've had to make do. A failed piece of equipment or unreachable digital tool is really no different than running out of markers, relying on old scales, showing a skip-prone CD, bad weather canceling an outside activity, etc.

Teachers are the most flexible people in the world for these very reasons (and thousands more like them). Don't forget your flexibility in other areas when you start to use technology. You're going to need it more than ever to serve your students well!

Back to the first point: respect. The atmosphere of mutual respect you build into your classroom environment means that when mistakes happen, they aren't to be laughed at, but corrected. Students need to respect the fact that everyone makes mistakes and they're part of the learning process. And guess what? That comes straight from the leadership you provide in your classroom. Your students will follow your lead in this area if you give them the chance. Building mutual respect as a ground rule means that when mistakes happen, everyone in the room treats them as natural moments to focus on, discuss, and ultimately solve.

Let the content drive the activity, not the tools. The question in your classroom should always be, "What are we learning today?" not "What tools are we using today?" Content is always king: the constant that should not be tampered with.

Yes, they will get excited about using Glogster or Timetoast, or Ning. But the point of the lesson is never to teach the tools themselves. You're not teaching Google Earth. Students are exploring weather patterns in different parts of the world. You're not teaching Google Docs, but rather encouraging your class to showcase their knowledge in a collaborative way. And, when your students compose and revise in the clouds, they are using another approach to analyze text and practice their writing skills.

Here's an eternal truth: Great teachers make great tools, not the other way around. Digital tools will only reach their learning potential when a teacher invests the effort to understand and use them as a means for their students to learn content. Keep your eye on the ball: students learning content.

My best teaching advice for mastery of these digital tools is to try as many out as possible, and take notes as you go. Each tool in this book includes a "Getting Started" section that leads you through your first steps in experimentation. If an idea for teaching content comes to you, jot it down within the book so you don't lose it. Once you've experimented with a good range of tools, go straight back to your content.

You'll start making connections almost immediately. If you teach science, online mind-mapping tools such as Webspiration may be a good fit for the time you spend on classification. If you teach math, creating screen recordings of difficult formulas or processes may jump out at you as being useful. If you are doing biographies as a language arts teacher, VoiceThread might click as a great avenue for allowing your students a new way to showcase their knowledge. By exposing yourself to a wide variety of tools, you will get better and better at making connections when you begin looking at the concepts your students need to grasp.

Start with Easy Technology Tools and Work Your Way Up. Have you ever felt intimidated while watching your more tech-savvy peers working on advanced technology projects? Does it seem like they're just wired differently than you? Well, I'm here to tell you that it's not true! Even the most tech-savvy teachers had to start somewhere, often with a simple tool matched to a simple lesson. The more they experimented, the further they stretched, and the easier it became to move to a more complex e-tool.

If you are new to digital tools, or if they have been thrust into your life with little support, starting with the "newbie" tools is the way to go. Match them with simple projects and lessons. Don't take on the largest and most difficult tools right off the bat, as this will likely only frustrate you and your students. Just follow the charts on p. xii to match your comfort level with lessons.

Get Connected with Your Own Personal Learning Network (PLN). Did you know that there are thousands of teachers out there waiting to lend you a hand or answer your questions? Or that the extra idea, resource, or support you need might be just a click away? Would you like the opportunity to collaborate easily with another class anywhere in the world?

It's all true! A personal learning network is exactly what its name implies: a network of people that you learn from, managed with the tools you select. Through the power of social networking and other online tools, educators all across the globe are connecting and offering each other support in not only the use of technology, but every other aspect of teaching and learning. Your PLN will become your way of sustaining the change you want to create for your students. A member of my own PLN, Mary Beth Hertz (Twitter ID: mbteach), summed the concept up perfectly on her blog, **www.philly-teacher.blogspot.com**:

A supportive and innovative PLN will help you grow in your career, help you grow as a person and give you a place to bounce new ideas around, ask simple questions or get help when you need it. It can also be a place of comfort and belonging when you feel isolated or alone.

So, how do you get connected and start building your personal learning network? First, get comfortable with some of the main e-tools: Ning, Twitter, and blogs. Each of these tools offer their own way to connect with passionate educators. Nings are safe social networking sites centered on topics that its members are invested in. To find educators like yourself, try one of these popular education Nings: The Educator's PLN (**www.edu-pln.ning.com**), or Classroom 2.0 (**www.classroom20.com**).

Each member of the Ning has a clickable profile that you can use to connect to his or her Twitter account and/or blog to enrich your connection. Within these groups, members pose questions, post resources, and provide support to other members. You can also head to the forums to see what topics are being discussed.

Although Twitter sometimes gets a bad rap for being frivolous, you'll find that most educators don't use Twitter to share about what they had for breakfast. When I log into Twitter, I see educators sharing ideas for teaching math concepts and encouraging discouraged colleagues to keep going. Active educators on Twitter build friendships and change lives for the better every single day.

I will caution, however, that participating in Ning, Twitter, or blogs can, at first, seem daunting. The amount of information available on these networks can seem like a flood. Start small and start smart. Don't "follow" the updates of hundreds of random people at once. Select perhaps two to five whom you admire. The list below is a good starting point: every one of these educators is passionate, provides great resources, and most importantly, is responsive. If you have questions or problems with using technology in your classroom, you couldn't ask for a better support system. To follow any of these individuals, go to his or her Twitter page (www.twitter.com/*TwitterID*) and click "Follow."

TWITTER ID

bethstill	hadlevjf	rmbyrne
blairteach	irasocol	russgoerend
brophycat	karlfisch	shellterrell
chrislehmann	kellyhines	smeech
clifmims	kjarrett	spedteacher
coolcatteacher	kylepace	stevejmoore
daylynn	larryferlazzo	stevekatz
dwarlick	mbteach	teachpaperless
edtechsteve (that's me)	mritzius	tgwynn
edutopia	msgregson	thenerdyteacher
ejulez	mtrump	tomwhitby
ewilliard	NMHS_Principal	twilliamson15
fisher1000	pammoran	web20classroom
geraldaungst	plugusin	woscholar

Remember, this list is just a *starting* point. As you get more comfortable with Twitter, you can also check out **www.twitter4teachers.pbworks.com**, which is a fantastic resource that sorts hundreds of educators by their main content area. Search Google for terms like "Math teachers on Twitter" or "Best teachers on Twitter" or any other search term. As you're searching, once you find an educator who brings value to you, click on their profile and click "following" to see who *they're* following. Chances are, you'll find some more excellent members.

Also, many educators offer suggestions on who to follow on Fridays (in Twitter, this is known as #followfriday or #ff). Always view and approve someone's posting history before you follow them, and don't be afraid to drop members if they don't add value to your experience.

If Twitter is too fast and furious for your taste, a blog may be a better fit for your PLN. Blogs offer insight that is typically more in-depth than the 140 characters that a tweet is limited to. The very first blog you need to follow is called, "Free Technology for Teachers," by US history and civics teacher, Richard Byrne (**www.freetech4teachers. com**). The second blog I'd suggest is my own (**www.edtechsteve.blogspot.com**), because it covers updates and new uses for classroom digital tools. I also provide more examples and details on how to integrate online tools into your classroom instruction routine.

There are many excellent lists of blogs for teachers. Each of the following lists include clickable links to blogs that you can easily scan to decide whether or not you'd like to subscribe.

Clear View Education, "100 Best Blogs for Teachers of the Future"
www.clearvieweducation.com/blog/2009/100-best-blogs-for-teachers-of-the-future

The Edublog Awards
www.edublogawards.com

Top 20 Teacher Blogs
www2.scholastic.com/browse/article.jsp?id=3752562

The best part of the PLN is the P—it is *personal*. You choose the tools, you choose whom to follow or not follow, and you choose how you want to interact on a daily basis. It is customized learning at its finest and most progressive, and you don't want to miss out, I promise!

So, get connected, start participating, and seek out the support you need to help change your classroom!

CHAPTER FOUR:
HOW TO ASSESS DIGITAL PRODUCTS

Checklists, rubrics, observations, student self-assessments, graded essays, and standard tests or quizzes are among the many assessment options you can use to assess e-tool products. Whatever tool you choose, here is some practical advice to help shape your assessment of the digital footprint you are helping your students create.

1. STUDENTS SHOULD IDENTIFY, INCORPORATE, AND ENGAGE THEIR AUDIENCES.

Because the products your students create will be published online and will become part of their digital footprints, how well the projects address their target audience should be the first assessment criterion. Encourage students to actively think about whom they are preparing the product for and what that particular audience may need to know.

Being attentive to an audience has always been an important part of assessment, but in the digital age, it's even more so. That's because the audience can talk back! Projects published on the Internet are not stagnant, unchanging pieces, and Internet audiences can take an active role in reshaping a product or in rating its value.

There are many examples of this. A video posted to YouTube, for example, can garner comments about the production values. The video creator then takes those comments into consideration and makes improvements, which are then commented on and possibly refined even further.

This back-and-forth between audience and creator happens in all kinds of areas, such as blog postings, wikis, VoiceThreads, and many more. The concept of the audience as an active and widespread partner in the publication process is unique to the digital age we live in and should be factored in when assessing student projects.

All it takes is a post with a link to your students' work and an invitation for others to take a look and offer input. You'll be surprised at how many will do so, and you will be greatly pleased when you see the reactions from your students. The minute they realize that their work is being viewed by an actual audience, they will work to improve it. Do not underestimate the power of allowing the public to consume and comment upon your students' creations!

> The minute your students realize that their work is being viewed by an actual audience, they will work to improve it.

From YouTube to blogs, from message boards to word clouds, the ability to have your work rated and commented on is quickly becoming standard practice. Peer and outside comments and ratings are some of the most powerful assessment tools for this generation of students.

Here are some questions that can help you understand whether or not your students targeted and considered their audience when creating their projects:

→ Who is the audience? Is it obvious? Why or why not?

→ Was the product geared toward the audience it was intended for? What proof is there of this?

→ Did the audience respond the way that students thought they would? If not, what was surprising and why did it surprise them?

→ Was the audience allowed an opportunity to have input into the project, either as it was being created or after it was finished? What changes were made because of audience comments or critiques?

→ Did the project reach as wide of an audience as expected? Why or why not?

2. MAKE SURE STUDENTS UNDERSTAND CONTENT AND CONNECT IT TO THEIR WORLD.

Simply put, the products your students create should show an understanding of content. Digital tools offer many opportunities for bells and whistles (animations, custom music, neat fonts, etc.), allowing students to show off their creativity in ways previously unheard of. This is a wonderful thing, as long as it does not overshadow the overall goal of showing what they know. Understanding, not special effects, should define a project.

Students also need to be able to connect the content they are learning to their world and their futures. The bottom line is that students need to be able to answer the fundamental (and often irritating) question, "Why do I need to learn this?"

There are several ways to make sure your students understand that what they are learning is important. The first is to anchor it with current events, either local or global. If you are focusing on soil and erosion, it may be good to identify examples within your community. If you are studying the American Revolution, make sure students can draw parallels to current events across the globe. Another way to promote connected learning is to place it within the context of their daily lives. If studying a novel, have students create products that show how certain characters are similar or different to themselves or people they know, for example.

These ideas are simply good teaching. They don't necessarily have anything to do with digital tools, and that is the point. Content is still king when assessing *any* product, whether it's published online or on paper.

3. LET STUDENTS REFLECT ON THE PROCESS OF CREATION.

As educators, we need to focus on creating a generation of flexible problem-solvers. What does this look like in the classroom? Frankly, it looks like a bunch of kids and their teacher creating projects, making mistakes, then collaborating to solve or work around the problems that arise within the process. Reflection is a huge part of this process, both ongoing and at the end of the publication of their product. When reflecting, your students should be answering these types of questions:

→ Did I address the essential content I was responsible for?

→ How well did I collaborate with my peers? How could I improve?

→ What issue or issues did I run into when creating my product? How did I solve this issue? Were there other ways I could have solved the same problem?

→ Did I connect to my audience? Why or why not?

→ Did my product garner wide attention and recognition? Why do some products gather more attention than others? How can I obtain an even larger audience for my next product?

→ Could I have chosen a better tool to show my understanding of this concept? Which tool and why?

→ How did the comments of others about my work affect the direction I took? Was this positive or negative? How will the comments of others about my finished product impact the next project I undertake?

4. ASSESS THE PRODUCT AND THE PROCESS, NOT THE USE OF THE TOOL.

We don't assess our students on the way they hold a pencil or how they flip pages in a book, and we've never assessed students on how well they push buttons on a calculator. It's the same for digital products, too. Keep the focus on content and the process, not the tool. Don't assess for a certain number of PowerPoint slides or the correct quantity of pictures, for example.

Thinking of technology as just another tool in our teaching arsenal helps us to move away from this type of assessment. On your rubrics, try to avoid phrases like, "Used X amount of photographs," or "Included at least one video." Instead, focus on their understanding of the content and the use of a good process to illustrate this understanding.

5. MAKE STUDENTS JUSTIFY THEIR CHOICES.

Students have a multitude of choices when they create their digital products, beginning with choosing the actual tool they decide to use. After that, they will choose what content to include and how to represent it–from color schemes, music, video clips, and much more.

Students should be able to justify the production choices they make in terms of how well the choices reflect the content and the audience. Keeping students focused on justifying their choices encourages them to be purposeful throughout each step of the creation process. Each choice they make should show what they know or say something about their creativity. Students should be able to answer the "why" along with answering the "what."

As you build this assessment component into your classroom, you will notice a shift in how your students approach the products they are to create. Instead of searching Google and copying the first picture they see, they will start looking for an image that best illustrates what they are trying to convey. Instead of randomly adding hearts and swirlies, you will see students adding creative components that make sense within the larger context of content and audience.

On the following page, you will find a sample rubric to use as a guide to construct your own. It incorporates the four points explained above. By the way, to create easy, customizable rubrics, I highly recommend RubiStar (**www.rubistar.4teachers.org**), which allows you to choose rubric templates or build your own printable rubric.

COLLABORATION

Category	4	3	2	1
Group Problem Solving	Actively looks for and suggests solutions to problems.	Refines solutions suggested by others.	Does not suggest or refine solutions, but is willing to try out solutions suggested by others.	Does not try to solve problems or help others solve problems. Lets others do the work.
Focus on the Task	Consistently stays focused on the task and what needs to be done. Very self-directed.	Focuses on the task and what needs to be done most of the time. Other group members can count on this person.	Focuses on the task and what needs to be done some of the time. Other group members must sometimes nag and prod to keep this person on-task.	Rarely focuses on the task and what needs to be done. Lets others do the work.
Mutual Respect	Actively seeks to incorporate other group members' opinions, ideas, or contributions.	Incorporates some of the other group members' opinions, ideas, or contributions into the project.	Recognizes the value of other group members' opinions, ideas, or contributions.	Puts down other group members' opinions, ideas, or contributions.
Value to Group	Routinely provides useful ideas when participating in the group and in classroom discussion. A definite leader who contributes a lot of effort.	Usually provides useful ideas when participating in the group and in classroom discussion. A strong group member who tries hard.	Sometimes provides useful ideas when participating in the group and in classroom discussion. A satisfactory group member who does what is required.	Rarely provides useful ideas when participating in the group and in classroom discussion. May refuse to participate.

CREATION

Category	4	3	2	1
Consideration of Audience	Strong awareness of audience in the design. Students can clearly explain how the choices they made fit the target audience.	Some awareness of audience in the design. Students can partially explain how the choices they made fit the target audience.	Students are able to describe the target audience and their needs, but project lacks evidence of this understanding.	Limited awareness of the needs and interests of the target audience. Cannot clearly identify their intended audience.
Justified Choices	Students are able to clearly link every design choice to content. Creativity is consistently shown in how the content ties into each choice.	Able to link most of the choices made to content. Can clearly describe decision-making process.	Able to link some of the choices made to content. Cannot clearly describe decision-making process.	Unable to justify any choices made.
Content Addressed Accurately	All facts are accurate.	99-90% of the facts are accurate.	89-80% of the facts are accurate.	Fewer than 80% of the facts are accurate.
Creativity Expressed	Product is easily identified as the creator's work. Can look at project and know who created it without asking!	Creator of the product can be identified somewhat easily. Audience is able to tell something about creator's personality.	Difficult to identify the creator of the product, but project is attractive and tells a little about the creator's personality.	Product shows little to no creativity. The project is dull and tells nothing of the creator's personality.

PUBLISHING

Category	4	3	2	1
Engages Audience	Reads and responds to all comments made about published work. Plans and implements multiple meaningful changes to incorporate feedback received.	Reads and responds to most comments about published work. Makes plans and implements one change to project based off audience engagement.	Reads and responds to some comments made about published work. Does not implement any changes to project.	Does not interact with intended audience.
Identifies Ways to Improve Next Project	Articulates a plan of attack for the next product that incorporates multiple lessons learned in this project.	Makes connections between mistakes made and lessons learned to utilize when creating next product.	Identifies mistakes made in the current project but cannot illustrate how these mistakes can be solved in the next product.	Cannot identify any way they will improve the next product.
Gives Appropriate Online Feedback to Peers	All feedback to peers on published products is clear, supportive, and provides direction on how the product can be improved.	Some feedback to peers on published products is clear, supportive, and provides direction on how the product can be improved.	Feedback is supportive but offers no direction to peers in how their product could be improved.	Feedback is not supportive.
Value to Group	Routinely provides useful ideas when participating in the group and in classroom discussion. A definite leader who contributes a lot of effort.	Usually provides useful ideas when participating in the group and in classroom discussion. A strong group member who tries hard.	Sometimes provides useful ideas when participating in the group and in classroom discussion. A satisfactory group member who does what is required.	Rarely provides useful ideas when participating in the group and in classroom discussion. May refuse to participate.

DIGITAL PORTFOLIOS

Great portfolios are not simply assessment tools, but learning tools as well. They become vehicles that your students use to begin thinking about their choices, mistakes, solutions, strengths, weaknesses, and how all of these elements mix together to present a picture of growth and progress.

A digital portfolio shares many characteristics of a typical portfolio. It is a collection of a student's work. The student assembles the portfolio over time, selects pieces from it, reflects on them, and uses them to illustrate his or her growth as a learner.

Digital portfolios differ from their traditional counterparts in two important ways: the targeted audience and the way they are published/presented. The traditional portfolio is a local document; students typically hand in work to a single teacher, or at most, a small panel of reviewers. In contrast, digital portfolios should be published for the world at large. Parents, community members, peers, and others in the online community should have the opportunity to view the progress and the thinking skills your students are developing. This wide, transparent audience will be a powerful motivator for your students.

As their name suggests, digital portfolios are not print products but are published electronically. They are housed on the Internet, where links, video, audio, images, and embedded files can be brought together in a central location. Each student has his or her own unique depository of products they select to represent their mastery of content and growth throughout the year.

The best tools for storing digital portfolios share important characteristics. First, the student should be able to access and save the tool from an Internet connection (i.e., saved to the Internet, not to a USB flash drive or single computer). The tool should be intuitive and allow students to embed or link to all the other e-tools they utilize during the year. It should also allow students to customize the look and feel of their portfolios. And, finally, your student should be able to upload their reflections via text, audio, or video with ease.

This book describes several tools that make excellent vehicles for this type of portfolio. They include wikis (p. 94), website creators (p. 92), Glogster (p. 50), Ning (p. 66), and Prezi (p. 70).

My personal preference is to have students create a website or wiki, because these are the easiest to set up and manage. They also allow students to start establishing their own personal, positive Web presence.

The process of setting up portfolio spaces is fairly simple. The first step is to establish a home site for each student. Using Weebly (a free website creator described on p. 92), for example, you would create accounts for each student. These accounts would then translate to their own unique site (e.g., stevejohnson.weebly.com).

Wikis work in much the same way. Each student creates a separate wiki space. Therefore, the first step is to guide students toward establishing their unique presence on the Web.

Then, you will want to have students structure their sites to meet your classroom needs. For example, if your class will be doing a lot of video products, students might create a "videos" page to deposit these items as the year progresses. If you will be relying heavily on digital storytelling, you may encourage students to create a page specifically for this purpose.

It's a good idea to model this process for students. Create an example or template ahead of time that shows the general outline of the points that will be asked of them. Setting these pages up on the front end will save time later when students begin to upload their products. They can always change or add pages to their portfolios as needed.

Once your portfolio spaces are set up online, here are some recommended strategies that you should consider when moving forward:

Recommended Strategy	Explanation
Allow students to choose the products they place into their portfolios	Not every product deserves to be placed into a student's digital portfolio. Rather, you should encourage your students to limit the number of entries and their corresponding reflections. This will help them to be more discerning about which products most effectively show their growth and mastery.
Introduce the concept of digital portfolios to all involved at the start of the year	During Open House, make it a special point to share with both students and parents what the portfolio looks like in your classroom and what will be expected. Answer any questions and give everyone a chance to give feedback as appropriate. Remember, transparency is key.
Have a scanner and digital camera available in your classroom	Having these items allows your students to quickly and easily digitize any offline products they are creating. Encourage students to be self-sufficient with these tools (i.e., if they want to include something they have done into their portfolios, they should know how to scan/take a picture of it and upload it to their portfolios without needing your assistance).
Create your own digital portfolio alongside your students	This is a great way to not only model what an effective digital portfolio looks like, but also to prove to your students that you are a learner throughout this process just as much as they are! Sharing your own growth as a learner will build a powerful collaborative relationship with your students that will pay off in many ways.

Show portfolios off to other teachers and administrators	Make sure to spread your student successes. This can lead to other teachers in the building taking a good look at implementing these techniques in their own classes. Be a leader!
Encourage students to connect their portfolios to social networking sites such as Facebook, Twitter, or MySpace	By posting links to their digital portfolios on the sites they already use to connect with peers and family members, students can reach a wide audience that they are already connected to. This inclusion of an authentic, connected audience will bring more feedback and lead to increased motivation and better products. Don't participate in the demonizing of these networks—get in the business of embracing them as the new way the world connects, communicates, and shares information.
Encourage peer assessment	Your students should be looking at, commenting on, and providing feedback to the portfolios of other students in the class (or in other class periods). Model good feedback and push students to take these comments into account when creating further products or reflection pieces.
Stay transparent and connect with parents	As a rule of thumb, any comments, reflections, or grades given to products should be published for all to see. Additionally, you should encourage parents to visit the site to give you and their student any feedback they can regarding the process or products being worked on in class.
Ask students to include product assessments as part of their portfolio	Your students should include a copy of the rubric that was used to assess each product included in their portfolio. This will shed even more light on their ability to grow as a result of your feedback on their products throughout the year.
Encourage students to not only include their best work, but also their worst	We learn most by the mistakes we make. Make sure students don't simply stick the prettiest or most complete products into their portfolio. Showing their mistakes and what they learned from them is even more important than showing off their best work. Always remind students that the purpose of the portfolio is to show both mastery and growth.
Keep high quality examples from year to year	Keeping portfolio examples from previous years will go a long way towards helping students visualize your expectations from the very beginning.

Have students present digital portfolios at the end of the year or semester	The culmination of the digital portfolio is a presentation by the student. Through this presentation, they should be able to prove both mastery of content and growth, as well as the process of creating a high quality product, how their thinking changed, how their ability to collaborate with others improved, and how well they connected to their audience as the year progressed. If possible, publish the student's presentation in some manner as well (with video or by Ustream-ing the event live).
Allow students opportunities to take their work with them	Through the use of digital portfolios, you are providing your students with an excellent opportunity to start creating a powerful digital footprint that they will carry with them. The worst thing you could do is require your students to establish this footprint in your class and then leave them with no opportunity to carry it with them in the future. In other words, do not delete portfolio sites at the end of the year! Allow students the opportunity to keep the site active by not deleting accounts, or otherwise allow them time to transfer files to a personal Web space.
Encourage students to share their digital portfolio with potential college admissions or employers	Fewer and fewer schools are relying solely on SAT Scores and grade point averages when selecting students. Including a link to an authentic digital portfolio could help your students stand out among other applicants.

As you begin to implement digital portfolios within your classroom, my hope is that you will see the power they have in unleashing your students' reflective abilities. Don't be afraid to learn right along with your students, and the possibilities for growth for both you and your students are endless!

PART II

DIGITAL TOOLS FOR TEACHING

TOOL #1

ANIMOTO

CONTENT AREA TIE-INS

Language Arts

→ Use for vocabulary terms and their definitions. Students research and upload pictures that represent the terms, then add text captions that describe the term and define it on each picture.

→ Use for literature response. Create a movie trailer for a book instead of a book report! Students can upload images and give snippets of information in the video that entices viewers to pick up the book.

→ Visually represent a poem. Have students break a poem down into sections or lines and find a picture online that represents each section. On the picture (within the video) students add text captions of the line it represents. Students can even use the highlight button to feature the line(s) of the poem that they felt touched them the most. Students should also pick music appropriate to the poem.

Math

→ Show steps involved with solving a problem. If you have a scanner available, students can write out the steps on paper to be scanned and uploaded into Animoto.

→ Solve specific math problems. Have students take pictures of themselves finding the volume of a jug or bucket and caption these photos with the mathematical concepts they applied. This same idea can be applied to other measurement concepts, such as finding the perimeter of their desks or the classroom, etc.

→ Create a video that introduces a math concept, such as different types of graphs, definitions of mean/mode/median, etc.

GOAL: TO EASILY PRODUCE A PROFESSIONAL-LOOKING VIDEO THAT INCORPORATES PICTURES AND MUSIC.

OVERVIEW

Animoto proudly proclaims itself as "the end of slideshows," and it does a good job of coming close to meeting that bold claim. Animoto offers an extremely easy way to produce professional-looking videos using photographs and illustrations that a student uploads to its site. The video can contain music using your own MP3 files or music that is available through Animoto. Once pictures and music have been selected and edited, Animoto does the rest by assigning transitions, adding effects, and publishing the video file.

BUT FIRST...

→ Because Animoto relies on Adobe Flash to function, make sure to install the latest version from the Adobe website (**www.get.adobe.com/flashplayer**).

→ Students must have some content to upload before they can create a video. Allow a day or two to research the content at hand and to download appropriate images, video, or music.

GETTING STARTED

Like many services, Animoto requires you to create an account. However, since you will be using this with students, it is highly recommended that you first apply for an educational use account. This type of account will allow your students (and yourself) to produce full-length videos and to download the videos as files (neither of which are available under a regular "free" account). To register in this way, go to **www.animoto.com/education**. The process requires you to provide your name, school, position, grades you teach, and a Web address.

Once registered, you are ready to create your own videos! Choosing a style of video is your first step (free styles include water, fire, earth, air, and color fold). Next up is to add images or video. You can do this by uploading straight from your computer, choosing from Animoto's gallery, or pulling pictures from other photo sharing accounts you operate online, such as Flickr, Facebook, SmugMug, Picasa, or Photobucket. After you upload the images and video, notice the editing options along the bottom of the editing screen. You will be able to add text, rotate, delete, duplicate, or spotlight (make one or more pictures featured within the video). When you are finished adding and editing, hit "Done." Next up is adding music. Select from Animoto's vast collection of clips or upload an MP3 file of your own. Once you have selected a song, click on "Save and Continue."

To finalize your video, select the length you desire (a "short" is thirty seconds and the maximum length is ten minutes). Add a title and description, and Animoto automatically produces the finished product. Depending on the number of images and the length of the song you selected, this final process can take several minutes.

Finally, Animoto offers clickable options at the top-right of the video to publish and share this finished video creation through Twitter, Facebook, MySpace, or with friends via e-mail. Your educator account gives you additional options to save the video as an MP4 file, embed the file to a blog or website, or remix the video. You can even order a DVD copy.

USE IN THE CLASSROOM

Digital video is an engaging and powerful tool that your students are most likely familiar with. This makes classroom use especially relevant and motivational. Videos can be used to convey information, provide creative outlets for students to express opinions, or spark discussion in the classroom. Students also have the option to comment on other videos produced in your classroom and beyond.

OTHER ISSUES TO CONSIDER

→ Have fun and let students be silly and creative when making movies! Movies can be used purely for fun, too: students could create an end-of-year movie of themselves and their friends, for example.

→ Animoto only accepts MP3 music files for upload. Therefore, iTunes songs will not upload to Animoto. However, it is possible to convert audio files from your computer to an MP3 format using a variety of free, downloadable programs. My two favorites are GoldWave (**www.goldwave.com**) and Audacity (**www.audacity.sourceforge.net**).

→ Remember to cite picture and music sources in a slide at the end of the movie or within the video's description.

→ The Educational Use account lasts for six months, then you will have to renew. Do this through "My Account" and don't wait until the last minute—do it a few weeks before the expiration date to keep your account set up and active. Mark your calendar!

I had grades 5, 7, and 8 use worksheets and online refrigerator magnets to create their own six-word memoirs. Once they had their words, they went online and searched for images. They needed to find two images for each word, and the visual representations that students used for words was very interesting. Using Animoto, students took their twelve images and added their six words. After choosing music, their videos were created.

CHRISTINA DIMICELLI
Computers/Technology

CONTENT AREA TIE-INS

Science

→ Ask students to graphically classify any biology topic, such as classifications of plants, animals, minerals, etc.

→ Produce videos about planets and their characteristics. This can be done in eight small groups within the classroom, or you can simply assign each student his or her own planet. Researched images and facts are inserted into the video as needed.

→ Produce a persuasive video on environmental topics that students can then share/publish. Topics could include effects of pollutants on the environment, the impact of an energy-efficient house, where local drinking water comes from/how it is processed, etc.

Social Studies

→ Create a movie about the country being studied in class with pertinent pictures and music.

→ Create a biographical movie featuring pictures and information relating to the subject, as well as music from the time period the person lived.

→ Create a movie that shows key aspects of a culture, including diet, family traditions, recreational pursuits, holidays, etc.

TOOL #2

BLOGS

CONTENT AREA TIE-INS

Language Arts

→ Encourage reflective writing about any and all topics in the classroom through blogging.

→ Pose questions on your blog associated with the reading(s) for the day or week. For example, ask the class why or why not they relate to a certain character.

→ Ask students to start and maintain a fictional blog from the perspective of a character in the novel you are studying.

→ Use blogs for researching authors, then have students report back interesting facts they have discovered.

→ Use blogs for researching authors or books being studied by having students search the Internet for blogs devoted to the topic. Better yet, find out if the author also maintains a blog— many young adult authors do, for example. Students then report on interesting facts they have discovered.

Math

→ Keep a math blog with students. Students "comment" about the lesson of the day and share the pieces they did or did not understand. Teachers follow up to answer questions and concerns.

→ Keep a "Problem of the Week" blog where a tough problem is posted, and students are able to "comment" their ideas and possible solutions.

→ Encourage student blogs that mentor other students. For example, students who excel in trigonometry can maintain a blog for others in lower grades who are currently taking the course.

GOAL: TO CREATE AN ONLINE JOURNAL THAT CONVEYS THOUGHTS, FEELINGS, AND CONSTRUCTS KNOWLEDGE.

OVERVIEW

In 1997, Jorn Barger blended the words "Web" and "log" and created the term "weblog" to describe an online journal for one's thoughts, feelings, and ideas. In 1999, online journal author Peter Merholz shortened the term to "blog." The simple notion of a blog has evolved over the years, with the result that today's blogs have many uses–from journalists posting in real time, to sites that review equipment or services, to blogs that take on a life of their own. When bloggers create public posts, they insert their ideas into the mass community, inviting comments and discussion.

BUT FIRST...

→ Research your school system's Web capabilities–most school website solutions now have a built-in feature to support classroom blogs. These may not be nearly as easy to use as the sites listed below, but they may be the only option allowed at your school (until you can convince your IT department to unblock some of the sites listed below).

GETTING STARTED

There are many ways to start blogging, and each has its pros and cons. The best way to see which service fits your needs is to go to each site and see some examples, possibly even registering at a few to try them out to see for yourself. Some of the more popular choices are Google's Blogger (**www.blogger.com**), WordPress (**www.wordpress.com**), and LiveJournal (**www.livejournal.com**). A popular choice for educators is Edublogs (**www. edublogs.org**) because it allows you to set up student blogs that are easy to manage and moderate.

No matter which blog site you choose, just create the site and start writing. The process is very similar to writing in a word processing document: you can edit fonts, colors, backgrounds, etc. You can also add images and video. Your blog will have a unique address (mine is **www.edtechsteve.blogspot. com**) that you can then share with colleagues, parents, or students.

At the end of your blog, you will have the opportunity to apply "tags"–those keywords associated with your blog that will cause your blog to show up in search results. For example, if I tag my blog with "educational technology," the blog will then show up in searches for "educational technology." This is a great way to direct traffic to your blog posts.

USE IN THE CLASSROOM

Blogs have many wonderful uses in the classroom. They can be an excellent communication tools for parents, students, and colleagues. Students can use them for research, or for private or public communication with teachers. Blogs encourage students to engage in meaningful writing targeted to a specific audience that is published in a public forum.

A classroom blog can also spark discussion both in and out of the classroom that can lead to a better learning environment for all involved. Any tool that encourages this much writing and reflection is a must in the twenty-first century teacher's arsenal!

OTHER ISSUES TO CONSIDER

→ Stay professional in all online interactions with students. Always remember that these interactions can be brought to the surface at any time.

→ Edublogs, mentioned above, is now easier than ever to use with students. As of August 2010, students do not need e-mail addresses to create a blog. This is a great help to students without an email account.

→ A blog can provide you with an important avenue for your own professional development. By seeking out and subscribing to blogs that pertain to your own educational interests, you can easily keep up with latest news and be exposed to the thoughts and ideas of others in your area.

→ Google Reader is a good site to manage your blog subscriptions (found at **www.reader.google.com**). With just a Google account, you can search for blogs related to your interests. Many bloggers also list the blogs that they follow as well, which can be helpful when you search and explore related blogs you would like to subscribe to. Once you subscribe to a blog, simply go to Google Reader, which will keep all of your blogs listed and provide you an easy place to read and manage content.

→ Feel free to drop by my blog at **www.edtechsteve.blogspot.com** to read and comment on anything you may find. I'm always looking for more educators to engage in conversation!

> When students are working on their blogs, I rarely have to help them and don't find myself having to ask students to get on task. The room feels high-energy with the buzz of science and tech talk.

ALPHONSO GONZALEZ
Science

CONTENT AREA TIE-INS

Science

→ Use blogs to record observations of experiments and new hypotheses that explain these observations.

→ Use a classroom blog as a digital display case for student projects. For example, you can post pictures to monitor student progress.

→ Use your classroom blog to keep students up to date on current events in science that are relevant to the topics at hand; for example, about the ongoing debate of Pluto's status as a planet.

Social Studies

→ Research and share blogs about current events with your students. Blogs are excellent sources of information, often unfiltered. They are also important pieces to use in discussions regarding media bias and the personal biases of bloggers.

→ Have students write blogs from the point of view of important historical figures they are studying.

COLLABORATIVE WHITEBOARDS

CONTENT AREA TIE-INS

Language Arts

→ Upload student stories for shared revision and editing as a PowerPoint slide or PDF document. Participants share ideas to improve the writing piece and make revisions with whiteboard tools.

→ Create and upload a PowerPoint that represents what the main character of the novel you are studying thinks and feels. Students can log in to ask this character his/her thoughts on different characters and events within the book.

→ Create an online book club. Offer the opportunity for students to log in regularly to discuss the latest chapter(s) the group has read.

→ Create pages with reading passages and ask students to reflect and respond collaboratively to text.

Math

→ Draw out math problems for participants to view, interact with, and solve.

→ Invite a former student to give a Web conference at the beginning of the year to preview the concepts new students will learn, and to share insights about the course. Allow your students the opportunity to ask questions and interact.

→ Provide a weekly "Math Help" night: an hour in the evening each week that allows students to log into your meeting and ask questions about concepts they're having trouble with. Use the whiteboard to illustrate the steps to solving problems.

GOAL: TO CREATE A ROOM ONLINE WHERE PARTICIPANTS CAN COLLABORATE WHILE UTILIZING A SHARED WHITEBOARD SPACE.

OVERVIEW

Collaborative whiteboards are one of the more recent, free Web tools. They allow users to create a room and invite others into it to share ideas. Think of it as the virtual version of inviting a group of students up to the board to work together on an idea. Users can draw, write text, upload images or hyperlinks, chat, and even see or hear each other through microphones and webcams. All of this takes place in real time over the Internet.

BUT FIRST...

→ These tools utilize Adobe Flash, so make sure this plug-in is updated on all the computers that will be involved in the meeting. You may want to include this info when sending out invites.

→ Always test your webcam (audio and video) before hosting a live meeting.

→ Be early! Always set up your virtual meeting at least ten minutes before the official start time. This gives you a chance to troubleshoot glitches, upload images, and welcome early arrivals.

→ Allow students an empty space to try out and play with these tools before you require them to work together. There is a big "wow" factor to these tools, and it's important to allow your students a chance to play around with them so they can get over the initial shock.

GETTING STARTED

There are many collaborative whiteboard solutions popping up these days. I recommend four highly useful, easy-to-use options:

1. FlockDraw (**www.flockdraw.com**): Great for lower-level students. Offers limited space and no chat or videoconference ability, but is highly intuitive and easy to use for elementary students.

2. Scribblar (**www.scribblar.com**): An excellent resource for uploading images, Scribblar allows multiple pages and the room is persistent (it saves information and stays online as long as you need it).

3. Dabbleboard (**www.dabbleboard.com**): Similar to Scribblar, but not as feature-rich or intuitive; although, it does allow you to create a room without signing up.

4. Dimdim (**www.dimdim.com/free**): An excellent, feature-rich tool. Its only major limitation is that the free version only allows twenty participants at a time.

Visit each of the tools first to decide which one fits best in your classroom. Each site allows you to create a test room or take a quick video tour to see what is offered. Look for overall ease of use, including when sharing the room link with students, uploading pictures and diagrams, keeping track of names/actions, and creating pages.

To fully test a collaborative whiteboard tool, you will need some people to collaborate with. I would suggest a small group of teachers, friends, family, or students. Simply give them the link, and ask them to log into the room and start drawing.

Once you have had some fun drawing with others via the Internet, you can try the other collaborative aspects of the site, such as chatting, and audio- and video-conferencing. Scribblar, Dimdim, and Dabbleboard all offer this functionality. They also offer the ability to upload images, which participants can draw or comment on. In addition, these three services provide an easy way to take a snapshot image of the whiteboard you and your students have been using, which can then serve as documentation of student work or be inserted into other projects.

USE IN THE CLASSROOM

There are many opportunities to use collaborative whiteboards with students, both locally and around the world. This could be a great tool for partnering with another class, as you can create a room to exchange ideas and build upon joint knowledge. It can also be utilized as a distance education tool. The interactive whiteboard is an excellent choice for "anytime and anywhere" meetings to share information. Real-time audio, video, and collaborative devices make collaborative whiteboards great tools for use both inside and *outside* the classroom.

You can also use these tools as a problem-solving vehicle. Just post your question or problem onto a whiteboard page and assign groups of students to log into the page to problem-solve or answer the question jointly.

OTHER ISSUES TO CONSIDER

→ Limit the number of students you allow to work on a page at a time. More than three or four can cause students to get in each other's way as they try to work on the task at hand.

FlockDraw turned a dull vocabulary lesson into a creative, collaborative masterpiece... This activity developed higher-level thinking skills as partners collaborated to determine which shapes to draw, who would draw them, and which tools were necessary in order to complete the task. The students were anxious to share their work with classmates via the interactive whiteboard.

SHERRY
Tech Facilitator

CONTENT AREA TIE-INS

Science

→ Use the webcam feature to show your participants an experiment. Explain each step and discuss hypotheses and conclusions via audio or written chat.

→ Use the Whiteboard feature to label parts of a diagram. When the image is uploaded, the Whiteboard feature allows you to draw on or create labels for each part.

Social Studies

→ Connect with students from the areas of the world you are studying. This can be initiated through ePals (**www.epals.com**), which is described on p. 48. Present information about cultural topics relevant to your students.

→ Ask students to "become" significant historical figures and conduct an online debate. For example, you could simulate the Constitutional Convention with students logging on as James Madison, Charles Pinckney, etc. Students can upload images of documents or supply links that support their positions.

→ Have students create their own flags in groups and explain the symbols they used. The flags could be of a country being studied, or an imaginary country located in the same area of the world.

→ Have students collaboratively label an uploaded map. This could be used for a wide variety of projects.

TOOL #4

DIGITAL STORYTELLING

CONTENT AREA TIE-INS

Language Arts

→ Pull a concept from a novel the class is reading, and ask students to create a movie that expresses that concept through pictures and music (themes such as good versus evil, betrayal, or loss).

→ Research a nonfiction subject the class is studying online. Students can download images and publish this information as a movie file.

→ Perform an author study and have students create a biographical movie to illustrate what they've learned.

→ Have students take lines of a poem and research images that represent each line. From this, they make a movie that shows what the poem means to them through images and accompanying music.

Math

→ Profile famous mathematicians and the contributions they made to the field by downloading images of their lives and writing facts about each.

→ Utilize pictures of graphs and ask students to add text or voice narrations to explain the graph type and what it represents. You can obtain graph pictures online or use the Print Screen feature to grab your own.

→ Have students upload pictures that represent fractions, shapes, angles, geometric concepts in nature, etc., to create, for example, a movie of pictures that represent symmetry or the Fibonacci sequence. Ask students to explain in text the meaning behind each picture.

GOAL: TO CREATE A MOVIE THAT TELLS A STORY FROM IMAGES, TEXT, AND MUSIC.

OVERVIEW

Digital storytelling is an easy way to integrate digital tools into your classroom. The basic premise is simple: tell a story through digital photographs and drawings, information, video, recorded voice, and music. This story can be based on anything you imagine, from a biography of a person, to a student-written creative piece, to a series of images that represent a poem, to a narrative that assembles information about a particular country or culture. The only limit to a digital story is the amount of imagination the teacher or student puts into the process!

BUT FIRST...

→ Locating the storytelling software that best fits your needs is the very first step. There are several good choices that are available for free. For PC users, the simplest and easiest to use is Microsoft Photo Story. Windows Movie Maker, which comes bundled with Windows, is another PC choice, although not as easy or intuitive as Photo Story. For Mac users, the iLife suite is bundled into the operating system. One component of the suite, iMovie, would be the choice here to create outstanding digital stories.

→ *Before* you throw your students on computers to start making their stories, carefully plan and research what content the students will be creating. It's important that students have researched their topic, downloaded pictures that will work for their story, and thought about sequencing issues before diving into the storytelling software. Providing this structure will allow students to deliver on the content while still being able to create something unique to their own style.

GETTING STARTED

Once your students are prepared and have a plan, the software facilitates their storytelling. Each program works roughly the same way: students import the pictures they have found, insert text on these pictures to describe the content, add music as desired, customize the whole production to suit their needs by adding transitions, effects, etc., and publish the story as a movie. Once the movies are created, I highly recommend that you find a way to publish these to the world, either via your school website or by uploading to video services such as SchoolTube (featured on p. 72 of this book) or even YouTube.

USE IN THE CLASSROOM

Digital storytelling is an effective tool because of its extreme ease of use and ability to present content in new, exciting ways. Both you and your students will be able to use these programs within minutes of opening them. This process can really bring topics to life! In our ongoing efforts to give students the opportunity to engage with their work, digital storytelling can be a vital resource.

OTHER ISSUES TO CONSIDER

→ Make sure to impress upon students the ethical responsibilities of citing picture and music sources when creating their movies.

→ Using personal music files can be a great touch and will bring many of your students into the creative process faster; however, listen to all songs for inappropriate material before allowing your students to use them.

→ When choosing music, make sure you emphasize to your students the appropriateness of the songs within their movies' overall context. In other words, Bobby McFerrin's "Don't Worry, Be Happy" might not be the ideal choice for a movie about the Civil War.

→ If any of these programs are not available to you in your school, don't hesitate to fight for them. The programs contained here are free, work easily on most computers, and have great educational value.

A fourth grade teacher at the Center for Early Education (where I work) gave an optional assignment for students to share something about their free reading book. As one option, students could work with me, the school's instructional technology facilitator, to make a "book trailer"—a book review resembling a movie trailer. Two girls chose this option... Everyone loved it! I immediately had requests from more students to help them learn to use Photo Story as well.

GAYLE COLE
Tech Integrator

CONTENT AREA TIE-INS

Science

→ Ask students to create an instructional video of how to perform a certain experiment by uploading pictures of themselves performing each step (digital camera needed).

→ Have students share their knowledge of the current topic by creating an informative movie (about the solar system, animal adaptations, moon phases, parts of a plant, etc.)

→ Have students upload graphs and record voice comments that narrate what is represented. If you have a scanner, students can scan in and upload their own graphs for their movie projects.

Social Studies

→ Ask students to create a movie biography of an important historical figure or event.

→ Download images of countries or regions, and students can provide information for each image with text captions or voice comments (with bonus points for incorporating a country's national anthem or other regional music to play alongside the images).

→ Have students illustrate their knowledge of mapping by showing images of maps and explaining the use of the map through caption or voice.

EPALS

Language Arts

→ Practice formal versus informal correspondence via e-mail.

→ Have students brainstorm important information about themselves that they would like to convey to counterparts from the other class.

→ Do a book study of the same novel with both classes offering opinions and insight.

→ Have students teach each other phrases in their native languages.

→ Find out if students speak different languages–messages in their native tongues can become a project for translation.

Math

→ Have each class research and present difficult word problems to each other, with students corresponding about strategies and solutions.

→ Working together, students obtain data about each other's culture and/or surroundings (average number of rooms in houses, number of TVs, number of siblings, etc.) Graphs are then created and exchanged to compare the data.

→ Have students of both cultures take and share pictures of objects in their school and/or neighborhood that illustrate geometric principles (e.g., symmetry, right angles, quadrilaterals, shape reflections, etc.)

→ Ask students to convert money from one culture to the other and discover what types of items they might be able to buy if they lived in their counterparts' locale.

GOAL: TO CONNECT WITH AND LEARN FROM STUDENTS AND TEACHERS ACROSS THE GLOBE.

OVERVIEW

Housed at **www.epals.com**, ePals Global Community is a community of teachers and students that connect students in classrooms across the world. Connections are initially made through safe and secure e-mail but can carry over to the sharing of pictures, video, audio, or even live teleconferencing. EPals offers incredible opportunities for students to make cross-cultural connections in our ever-flattening world.

BUT FIRST...

→ Contact your IT department or administrative team to determine what policies are in place for exchanging student pictures and e-mail addresses, conducting teleconferences, etc. Make sure to follow these guidelines closely.

GETTING STARTED

As with most online services, registration is the first step. Once registered, the very first thing you will want to do is create a highly descriptive public profile, which allows other teachers to find out your location, what types of students you teach, their age range and interests, and a number of other key pieces of information. The better and more descriptive your profile, the better chance you will have of successfully connecting with another class.

Depending on your needs, you may decide to create student e-mail accounts that your students can use to correspond with other students across the globe. Creating monitored accounts is easy, and you can feel safe knowing that these accounts are completely safe, as you will have the chance to read and approve every e-mail sent to your students. This is the case on the other end of the connection as well, creating a well-moderated dialogue.

After setting up accounts, you will browse through the main ePals homepage for classes to connect with. To start, select "Collaborate," which bring up four ways to search for classes: by "Classroom Profiles," "Country," "Project" or through the teacher forum. The first allows you to specify search criteria, while searching by country allows you to browse class profiles through a world map. Searching by project is the most recent addition to the ePals site. It offers a chance to join into a global, shared project framework (such as a global book club, water projects, or global warming) for all involved classrooms. Finally, the teacher forum is a place where teachers from around the world post messages and actively look to connect with other educators.

After you find a good match, simply click on the "Contact" button to initiate contact with the teacher of that class. If he or she responds quickly, you are on your way! If there is no response, find another match and attempt to make contact again.

USE IN THE CLASSROOM

The potential for greater cultural understanding through the use of ePals is enormous! What better way to motivate students to learn about another culture than to actually interact with members of that culture? This can lead to not only a greater understanding of one another, but also a greater appreciation for similarities and differences. ePals also offers your students the chance to write for a real, authentic audience through e-mail correspondence.

Of course, e-mail correspondence is just the beginning. The ability to collaborate on projects is a key feature as well. The first correspondence in the relationship is teacher-to-teacher, so with this partner you can build the project into whatever shape your imagination allows. Perhaps you will work together to look at data, discuss a current event that affects both cultures, prepare presentations to inform, or even schedule a live conference in which students get the chance to come face-to-face. The choices are limitless!

OTHER ISSUES TO CONSIDER

→ Don't be discouraged if you don't get an immediate response. Differing time zones or school schedules may be the reason. It is often better to go "on the hunt" yourself rather than sitting and waiting for a class to find you.

→ If you stage a webcam session with another class, make sure you prepare well with the other teacher so that the students have something to do. In other words, don't just turn the webcam on and say, "Hi." Most students will naturally be shy unless they have been prepared with some material to work on beforehand.

> The students like the English language a lot when they use this tool. They understand that it is more than a subject at school. They force themselves to develop their English skills in a very secure environment. Also, they are more motivated when I teach in the classroom. They are more excited about learning English, and they are more careful when they are writing and speaking English....

IREM EBRU GURSOY
English

CONTENT AREA TIE-INS

Science

→ Inquire about and record weather data for the other locale and make inferences and predictions based on the information gathered.

→ Ask students from each class to come up with a favorite experiment that they have done in the past and would like the other class to perform and comment upon.

→ Have students send each other a weekly log of food/calorie intake and compare results.

→ Discuss and explore the local effects of global warming, erosion, or climate in general; for example, how do climates influence our daily lives?

→ Share pictures and/or short videos of different animals that are local to each classroom's environment.

Social Studies

→ Have students ask and answer questions, as they are face-to-face with another culture.

→ Discuss the economics of each local culture: What is the standard of living in both places? What types of goods and services are available?

→ Enrich the experience through a webcam session in which each classroom is responsible for teaching the other about key historical moments in their country.

Language Arts

→ Give students poems and ask them to represent them through Glogster (the less direction given for this, the more creative your students will be!)

→ Ask students to create a fictional product that they would like to sell and then produce a Glog to market it.

→ Have students create and illustrate poetry or book reports using Glogster.

Math

→ Have students demonstrate their knowledge of fractions by dividing a Glog up into equal fractional parts and working out different problems (adding, subtracting, reducing, etc.) in each part.

→ Ask students to search for and import videos from SchoolTube that show how to solve problems similar to the types you are working on. Import the videos into a Glog and ask students to add text or recorded audio describing the process in their own words.

→ Ask students to create a Glog with a coded message using symbols and graphics instead of letters. See if they can decode each other's Glogs.

GOAL: TO CREATE AND SHARE AN ONLINE MULTIMEDIA POSTER THAT CAN INCLUDE TEXT, GRAPHICS, IMAGES, VIDEO, AND AUDIO.

OVERVIEW

Glogster is a great way to create Glogs, or interactive posters filled with multimedia objects that are very easy to add and edit. Those who post them are known as Gloggers. Most Gloggers are teens and pre-teens who have found a way to express themselves in creative ways using images, video, audio, text, and graphics. These creations are then published and shared in a variety of ways.

Glogster is also a social networking site where you can friend other Gloggers, leave comments, send messages, and rate your favorites.

BUT FIRST...

→ Make sure to check to see if your school's filter blocks Glogster. If Glogster is blocked, refer this site's information to your IT department so they have the tools to unblock the "EDU" portion: **www.howtounblockglogsteredu.com**.

GETTING STARTED

Glogster offers a special "EDU" version that is great to use with students. Because the EDU version is moderated, students are not subject to exposure to inappropriate content. You can register at **www.edu.glogster.com**. One great feature of Glogster EDU is that it allows you to create up to two hundred student accounts. When you specify the number of accounts you need, Glogster will send you an e-mail with all of the usernames and passwords. I strongly suggest that you print this list as a reference.

By the way, be sure to always create more accounts than you need when you register. It's always good to have some backups in case you get more students in your class or one of the usernames you are given does not work correctly.

The great thing about setting up student accounts through Glogster is that students get the very same functionality of the tool in a safe environment, moderated by you, the teacher. Within their school's account, students will only be able to view, comment on, or rate the Glogs created by the other students in your domain.

Once you and your students are successfully logged into Glogster, the next step is to create your first Glog. Just click on "Create a New Glog" to get started. You will be presented with a pre-made Glog that you can change in any way. You can delete objects by clicking them and then clicking the trashcan (or hitting the delete key).

To add your own objects, ideas, and colors, click on the object you would like to add in the floating black toolbox on the left-hand side. This is also where you add text, images, graphics, video, audio, or change the "wall" or background of your Glog. For example, through an exclusive partnership with SchoolTube, video can be uploaded or imported from **www.schooltube.com** (featured on p. 72).

Each element is easy to manipulate across your poster; you can layer them so that they lay on top of or behind other objects. Images can be uploaded from your computer or selected from a public gallery. Each element can be resized, rotated, or otherwise customized.

When your Glog is finished, it is time to publish and share it. To do this, click the "Save and Publish" button. You are then presented with three options: publish as a gift, a greeting, or a classic Glog. You can experiment with all three, but the classic Glog will probably be the type you use most often (the first two types are meant for sending to an individual, the third is meant for publishing for public view.)

You are then prompted to name the Glog, put it into a category (such as "love," "music," or "school") and apply tags or search terms that others can use to find it later. After entering this information, click the "Save and Publish" button. This saves your work and gives you a direct link to your Glog that you can send to others. You can also post the Glog to Facebook, MySpace, Bebo, Yahoo!, Ameba, Blogger, and many other sites.

USE IN THE CLASSROOM

Glogs are *excellent* outlets for creative expression. Students really get into the idea of creating an interactive poster that they can fully customize in any way they see fit. This tool also incorporates the powerful aspect of publishing in a variety of formats. Students really like the fact that they can direct friends, family, or anyone they like to see their creation. Glogster can be used to present information on any and all subjects in a safe, creative environment. Your students will love this tool!

OTHER ISSUES TO CONSIDER

→ Be warned: the regular **www.glogster.com** is an angsty, creative teen outlet. Anytime you give young people an opportunity to wear their hearts on their digital sleeves, you will find drama!

→ Remember to have your students cite sources as needed, perhaps in the description section of each Glog.

→ Each object within a Glog can become a link by clicking "Edit" when the object is selected, then clicking on the hyperlink button. This allows students to create links to other websites that offer more information about a topic.

I had my students pick a human rights violation from the area of Africa or Asia, then research details about it. Instead of having them do a paper on it, I asked them to do a Glog... The projects I got back were powerful, and the students were impacted. I witnessed student researching harder than they had previously... They were using high-level skills that I could not get out of them in a traditional paper format.

BERNARD WAUGH
Social Studies

CONTENT AREA TIE-INS

Science

→ Ask students to create a Glog that shows the process of an experiment they performed in class. If possible, include actual photos of the students working through the experiment.

→ Have students create an animal classification poster, complete with images and videos of the animals being represented.

→ Have students conduct research about an area of land that has changed over time. Ask them to produce a Glog that shows the changes and explains why they occurred.

Social Studies

→ Have students focus their Glogs on an important invention and its impact on society.

→ Create a "Wanted" poster for a historical figure that did harm to others or his or her country.

→ Have students create a Glog that shows what they could buy for the equivalent of $100 in another country.

GOOGLE DOCS

Language Arts

→ Create a journal document for each student that is only shared between you and that student. Here, students can ask questions and receive answers from you with privacy assured.

→ Create and share a compare/contrast document. Assign one group of students to outline similarities between the two topics (whether it be book characters, genre types, authors, poetry passages, etc.) and the other to outline differences.

→ Create a collaborative story that reaches beyond the walls of the classroom. Ask students to begin a story and then post it as a Google Doc, inviting all to participate. Watch the story grow and change and check on it periodically as a class to see how it has evolved.

Math

→ Upload and share a test you have already given the students and ask them to work together to improve it. Take feedback and discuss changes they have made and why these changes may or may not be incorporated into the next test that is given.

→ Provide a spreadsheet with raw data and assign different groups to create charts using the same data. Discuss whether or not one type of graph makes more sense than another.

GOAL: TO COLLABORATIVELY CREATE AND EDIT PRESENTATIONS, SPREADSHEETS, AND WORD PROCESSING DOCUMENTS.

OVERVIEW

One document with multiple authors and readers sums up Google Docs, which represents a large leap forward in terms of the ability to collaborate in real-time on documents over the Internet. The idea is straightforward and powerful: two or more people from anywhere in the world can have the same document open. When one person makes a change, the document is automatically saved and updated for every person viewing it. Changes can be made in real-time among collaborators, and the document resides "in the clouds" (i.e. on the Internet).

Real-time collaboration on a single document is extremely powerful when you consider how most work is still done today: one person creates a document and e-mails it to another who then adds more information and e-mails it back to the first person with a new document name, and on and on. With Google Docs, reading, editing, and revising is as simple as creating or uploading a document and then inviting others to participate in the process.

BUT FIRST...

→ Google Docs will not work with Internet Explorer 6 any longer. If this is the version your school system uses, consider using another browser such as Firefox (**www.mozilla.com/en-US/firefox/firefox.html**) or Google Chrome (**www.google.com/chrome**).

GETTING STARTED

You will need a Google username for Google Docs. This is a great account to have anyway, since Google has many tools for both education and personal use that are unlocked simply by creating an account. Once you create your account, go to **www.docs.google.com** and sign in.

Once inside Google Docs, you can start working on a document by either by creating a new document or uploading one that you previously created. To create a new document, click on "Create new," and pick which type you would like to try (Document, Presentation, Spreadsheet, Drawing, or Forms. Google Forms is covered on p. 56.)

Once you click on one of these options, a new blank document will be created, ready for you to play with. If you would rather start with something you have already created, click on the "Upload" button. You can upload word processing documents, PowerPoint presentations, or Excel sheets. To import your file into Google Docs, simply click "Upload" and "Select files to upload." Then click the "Start upload" button.

Once you have a document open, play around with the environment so you get a feel for how to do things within Google Docs. The menus, along with most of the buttons along the top of the document window, are straightforward and should be familiar if you've worked with Microsoft Office products.

Finally, we arrive at the part that truly separates Google Docs from the pack: Sharing. Just click the "Share" button when you are ready to have another person view or work on it.

From here, you can share the document in several ways. You can e-mail the document to others as an attachment or publish it as a webpage (free, supplied by Google). This webpage is not editable by those who view it, but it can be a quick and easy way to share work. If you want others to collaborate with you on the file, click "Sharing Settings." This is where you can give others access to edit the document. You can do this by sending individuals an invitation through their e-mail (which does not have to be Gmail), or by publishing a link to the document. This link can be made private or public. Lastly, you can publish the document as a All of these sharing options will take some exploration and trial and error.

USE IN THE CLASSROOM

The powerful collaborative features of Google Docs make it an amazing tool to use with students. Groups can work together on the same document in real time. The document is stored online at Google Docs and is automatically saved every time it is changed, so no more worrying about lost files! When a document is finished, it can be published right from Google Docs as a traditional document. For example, if you create a presentation in Google Docs, you can save it as a .ppt file. Or, the presentation can be shared/published as a Web page with its own unique link.

It is very easy to track the specific revisions that each student makes, too. When the document is open, click on "File" and go to "See Revision History." This helps to track who has contributed what to the project. It also allows you to revert to an earlier version of the document, just in case a student accidentally wipes something out unintentionally. With all of these features (and more added all the time), Google Docs is a tool you cannot afford to overlook!

OTHER ISSUES TO CONSIDER

→ Google Docs can also be an invaluable planning tool within grade level teams or subject area groups. Collaborate on creating shared assessments, shared lessons, shared presentations, etc.

→ There are many templates available to you within Google Docs. To access these, go to "Create new" and click on "From template…." A searchable list of templates uploaded by users will appear. Before starting your own document, check and see if someone out there has already finished it and has offered it up for the taking.

→ Google Docs now supports the use, management, and sharing of entire folders of documents. This makes collaborating on multiple related documents much easier.

→ You can also utilize Google Docs as personal online file storage, since it gives you 1 GB of space. This means that instead of a flash drive, you can store your documents online and access them wherever you have Internet service.

CONTENT AREA TIE-INS

Science

→ Track weather patterns with a spreadsheet that students are responsible for updating each day.

→ Using experimental data, create a master spreadsheet that students can edit with the observations and measurements they make. All data is collected in one place and can then be analyzed as a class or in small groups.

→ Have students inventory your equipment by creating and sharing a spreadsheet that they complete.

Social Studies

→ Collaborate on a document with others from around the world.

→ Have students research a current event (local, national, or global) and determine a stance. Group students according to stance and allow them to collaborate on a Google Docs presentation that states their case. When finished, publish this document and send it to actual stakeholders in hopes of a response.

→ Create a blank timeline with important dates listed (but no events). Share this document with students, and allow them to race to find what events happened on each date and update the document with the answers.

TOOL #8

GOOGLE EARTH

CONTENT AREA TIE-INS

Language Arts

→ Use Google Earth to actually see and explore settings for historical fiction and non-fiction works.

→ Ask students to locate what they believe to be a spot in the world they would most like to live. Ask them to write descriptive paragraphs explaining why they chose that particular spot.

→ Visit Google Lit Trips (**www.googlelit-trips.com**). As a LA teacher, you won't want to miss this site; it offers fantastic maps that pair great K-12 literature with Google Earth, bringing the settings of many classics to life for students!

→ Have students create a travel brochure for a spot they have explored and enjoyed within Google Earth.

Science

→ Ask your students to choose a random city in another continent and try to guess what types of weather they experience based on their global positioning, surrounding landforms, proximity to water, etc. Then turn the Weather layer on to find current and average temperatures and rainfall.

→ Track hurricanes under the Weather layer.

→ Explore earthquakes and volcanoes through their respective layers under "Gallery." Use that in discussions about why earthquakes are common in some places and not others.

→ Turn the NASA Earth City Lights layer on under "Gallery" to see their great satellite pictures and information about all kinds of weather phenomena, including tornadoes, hurricanes, floods, etc.

OVERVIEW

Google Earth is an amazing program that continues to present new and powerful uses. At its heart, it is a simulation of the Earth based on publicly released satellite images. Within Google Earth, you are able to go anywhere in the world and zoom in to take a closer look at the streets, objects, and even people contained in these static satellite images. Users can search and explore mountain ranges, small towns, big cities, farms, polar icecaps, and everywhere else you can imagine.

But this is only scratching the surface of what Google Earth allows you to discover. By applying different layers on top of the Earth, you can find practical information about the locations of schools, hospitals, restaurants, churches, banks, much more. You can also find active volcanoes, tourist attractions, hurricane tracks, climate information, and much more. Other layers allow you the ability to see photographs uploaded by users throughout the world, providing a visual to accompany the satellite imagery. What's more, Street View (under the "Layers" panel) places you at a site and provides a panoramic view of the location. As if this wasn't enough, Google Earth now offers the ability to explore Mars, the Moon the constellations, and the depths of the ocean–all from within this one stellar program.

BUT FIRST...

→ Make sure all participating computers have Google Earth installed with the latest version.

→ Build some playtime into your first Google Earth lessons. It's important to give students some time to explore this software before they use it strictly for content.

GETTING STARTED

Google Earth is completely free and available for download at **www.earth. google.com**. After installing the free download, the world is at your fingertips... literally! Open Google Earth and start exploring. Navigation is easy. Use your mouse to click and drag to different areas of the globe and use your mouse wheel to zoom in and out. In addition, you can hold the mouse wheel button in and drag to tilt your view of the Earth.

Typically, the first search you and your students will do when starting Google Earth for the first time is finding their houses. This is good practice and is easy enough to do. Simply enter an address into the "Fly To" bar in the upper left-hand side of the screen. Here, you can also enter any address, city, or country and you will automatically be taken there. Once there, you can zoom in and out to see the area up close or further away.

After you've found your house and explored your hometown, you are ready to venture out into the world. One quick way to see some of the more famous places in the world is by opening the "Sightseeing" category under the My Places folder. Here you will find a list of sites such as Mount St. Helens, the Eiffel Tower, and the Red Square in Moscow. Simply double-click to fly to each of these places. It is also recommended that you make sure "3-D Buildings" is turned on under "Layers", as this allows students to see simulations of buildings placed on top of the map in scale.

After doing some sightseeing, it is time to explore the most powerful part of Google Earth—the Layers. This is located on the left-hand sidebar and contains many categories. Each category produces an overlay, or layer, on top of the Earth. Multiple layers can on at one time. Open up each category that interests you and click to turn some of these layers on. Ones you don't want to miss are Weather, Gallery, Geographic Web, and Places of Interest. There are many layers that offer educational value—explore and make these discoveries as you go.

When you are finished exploring the Earth, it is time to blast into space and try out Google Sky. This is represented by a button at the top of the screen that looks like Saturn. Here, you can explore and learn about stars, galaxies, constellations, planets, and more. After Google Sky, check out the "Red Planet" Mars and our very own Moon. Each of these offers a ton of information and amazing imagery that simulates these surfaces based on public satellite images.

USE IN THE CLASSROOM

It would take an entire book to speak to the countless uses that Google Earth can have in your classroom. The program is so easy to use that students and teachers alike have little problem getting the hang of it. From novel settings to explorations of the polar ice caps, Google Earth has much to offer every content area.

OTHER ISSUES TO CONSIDER

→ The images in Google Earth are not in real time. Students will inevitably ask if they are being watched, and the answer is no!

→ When you or your students find notable places you would like to save, add a thumbtack by clicking on the thumbtack button at the top of the program. For the tack to save upon exiting the program, you will need to name it and place it on the map. You can also customize thumbtacks by changing colors, styles, icons, etc.

→ You can save Google Earth images as JPEGS to embed into any other type of project you are working on (presentations, posters, or many of the other tools found in this book). To do this, go to File/ Save/ Save Image. To ensure you're following proper guidelines for the use of these images, read this page: **www.google.com/permissions/geoguidelines.html**.

→ Go back in time and view historical imagery. Simply click the clock button at the top of Google Earth and a time slider will appear where older images are available.

→ When visiting the Moon simulation within Google Earth, be sure to check out the layer that illustrates all of the different moon landings, where they were, who took part, and what was collected there.

→ Virtual tours created by many Google Earth users provides focused information on a wide range of subjects, from stadiums to museums to much more. Start exploring these tours by going to **www.earth.google.com** and clicking the "Gallery" link. To start a tour, click on the "Open in Google Earth" link, and the tour will automatically load.

CONTENT AREA TIE-INS

Math

→ Find the distance between any two points, or create your own path using the ruler tool at the top of the screen.

→ Use the ruler tool to figure out the perimeter of your school, county, or state. Have students find this individually, then cross-reference each other to see if they agree. Discuss why numbers may be off and take averages to approximate your best guess.

Social Studies

→ Turn the latitude/longitude grid on by going to View, then "Lat/Lon Grid". This turns these directional lines on and allows you to zero in on specific points just by referring to their positional data. Give students quizzes in which you give coordinates for them to look up.

→ Make current events come to life by showing students exactly where the event is happening on the globe. Do this daily, weekly, or monthly.

→ Explore any country in the world you are studying in myriad ways: through satellite imagery, digital photos, street views, etc.

→ Turn the National Geographic layer on to see their articles about places all over the world.

→ Utilize historical map layers to see the world through the eyes of people who lived during those times (find these layers under "Gallery" and then under "Rumsey Historical Maps").

→ Turn the "Google Book Search" layer on under the "Gallery" category to explore written historical documents from different parts of the world.

→ Turn on the US Government layer under "More" to learn more about senators and representatives from across the country.

GOOGLE FORMS

CONTENT AREA TIE-INS

Language Arts

→ Collect data about student reading habits (frequency of reading outside of school, what genres are their favorites, whether they would rather read the book or see the movie, etc.) This could be an interesting survey to take to the community at large as well.

→ Have students create an online quiz about the novel you are reading. Students can form groups and come up with questions, and then the whole class takes the quiz upon completion of the book.

→ Use Forms for students to complete book reports online.

Science

→ Have students create a form to take out into the community about the types of recycling that people are now doing. Ask students to put the word out to family members and friends to increase the amount of data.

→ Survey students from throughout the school about their healthy (or unhealthy) eating habits at school. Ask what types of lunches they typically eat, what items they typically purchase, etc. Students can analyze this data and provide the school population with a chart of calories, sugar content, etc. that can help their peers make better choices. Run the survey again later in the year to see if their efforts made a difference!

GOAL: TO EASILY CREATE SURVEYS OR TESTS THAT ARE AUTOMATICALLY INSERTED INTO A SPREADSHEET TO COLLECT AND ANALYZE DATA.

OVERVIEW

Google Forms is a part of Google Docs, a larger set of tools outlined on p. 52 of this book. By itself, it is a tool for creating and sharing surveys in order to collect, analyze, and represent data. Multiple question types are supported to gather a wide variety of data; many themes are provided to create an attractive survey; and surveys are easily published. The best part, however, is that the collected data is automatically placed into a Google Docs spreadsheet, which can then be used to analyze results, create graphs, and export as an Excel file, PDF, or Web page for easy viewing.

BUT FIRST...

→ You will need a Google Account to access this tool. See the "Google Docs" tool on p. 52 for information on setting up your account.

GETTING STARTED

To get started with Google Docs, log in to your Google Earth account by going to **www.docs.google.com** and signing in. Or, go to **www.google.com** and sign in, then head to "My Account."

Once inside, you can create your first survey. Simply go to 'Create new" and click on "Form." A window opens titled "Edit form," from where you can begin adding questions. You will want to give your form a title and, underneath it, include some directions to your audience as to what you are looking for.

Each question box allows you to choose from seven different types of question/answer formats: text, paragraph text, multiple choice, checkboxes, choosing from a list, grids, or scales. I encourage you to try them all out when you first begin playing around with your own forms. Once you choose a question type, you can then insert the question along with any help text you would like to include and the answer choices (if applicable).

Before clicking "Done", you can check whether you want this question to be a required response. For example, if the first response you want is the user's name, it is a good idea for it to be required. When you click Done, you are presented with another question to insert, and the question you just entered will show as it appears on the form. You can also add new questions by clicking on the "Add Item" button at the top of the form.

When your survey contains the questions you want, click the Theme button to tailor how the survey looks. Try some out until you get the look/feel you want.

Once your survey is ready to use, you have two ways to publish it. The first option is to e-mail it by clicking on the "E-mail this form" button. You will be able to e-mail accounts here by simply hitting Send. Or, people can access your survey through a link that you copy, paste, and post to a website. The link is at the very bottom of the screen.

Once people are directed to the link and take your survey, it is time to check on results. To do this, log back into Google Docs and click on the link for the form you created. This will take you to a real-time spreadsheet with all responses contained within. You can then use this spreadsheet to share with students, create graphs, and otherwise analyze the data you have received.

USE IN THE CLASSROOM

Data collection is a key component in any high-quality classroom. Google Forms can be an easy way to collect data about all kinds of topics (elicit information from students about the classroom environment, what types of foods they eat and games they play, how many hours a day they read, etc.) You can also use these forms as great bridges between home and school. For example, you can elicit information from parents regarding their child and how they feel the class is working for them.

The way that data seamlessly flows into the Google Docs spreadsheet is also a powerful tool because the spreadsheet makes it easy to dissect and analyze responses and predict future results. It also provides a great platform for discussion about "real" data with students. You can also utilize these forms from year to year to study a topic longitudinally–for example, how did one class differ from another and why did they differ? Finally, you can also use these forms as online quizzes or tests. The responses will feed directly into a spreadsheet that allows you to easily see problem areas to further work on with your students.

OTHER ISSUES TO CONSIDER

→ There is no real way to stop a respondent to a form from putting in a false name and putting in false information. The good news is that you control the spreadsheet and can delete any suspicious entries before students ever see the data. Monitoring is key.

→ You, as the creator of the form, are the only one with access to the survey results. They are not published or displayed unless you choose to do so. Because of this, the data you collect can either be kept safe and anonymous, or you can choose to publish the results.

→ Google Forms is easily viewable on mobile devices such as the iPod touch, iPhone, and Android. If your school has access to a cart of these devices, this could be a very easy way for your students to take quizzes and tests.

→ When sharing data, be sure to think carefully about how you want to share results. You can share a spreadsheet that forces users to log in with a Google account to view the spreadsheet. If you choose this option, the person you are sending it to must have a Google account. You can also choose whether or not you want to give edit rights to those you share the document with.

CONTENT AREA TIE-INS

Math

→ Create forms that coincide with statistics experiments. Have students enter data about a number of trials and the outcomes of each trial. This data is then automatically populated into a spreadsheet for easy analysis.

→ Put math into real context by creating a survey asking students about their daily living habits: how long they watch TV, stay on the computer, chat with friends, ride a bike, play sports, etc. When data is collected, students tally the totals, find averages, and create graphs based upon what they have found.

→ Create a survey intended for parents that asks their thoughts and feelings about math in general, and specific math topics in particular (feelings about fractions, long division, statistics, etc.) Have students complete the same survey and then compare results to their parents. Perhaps form a support network among the class (and parents) for different topics (i.e. if one student or parent is strong in a particular area, her or she could be a resource to others that are weak).

Social Studies

→ Have students create a form for parents, aunts, uncles, and grandparents. Students can ask about the activities that each of these relatives participated in when they were the same age as the student. When data is collected, analyze it as a class based on the time in which the respondent lived and put results into historical context.

→ Create a form to survey people in the country you are currently studying. Attempt to acquire data from people in this country by connecting via ePals (**www. epals.com**), which is detailed on p. 48 of this book.

IMAGE EDITING & ENHANCEMENT

CONTENT AREA TIE-INS

Language Arts

→ Have students upload photos of themselves at various ages, then caption them with biographical information.

→ Have students research and upload pictures that match what they envision the setting of a book they are reading looks like. They should caption the title of the book and note what page number describes the scene they have tried to capture.

→ Ask students to find a picture of a particular type of setting and then write a short paragraph that describes the setting. Afterward, students upload this picture and distort it using image effects. Other students then load the picture on their computers and attempt to describe the new setting. Compare the descriptions of the settings before and after the photo was distorted within the editor.

Math

→ Ask students to find photos that illustrate mathematical concepts (or to take their own during field trips). Examples include tall buildings (multiplication), honeycombs (patterned sequences), racecars (acceleration/velocity), etc.

→ Have students create photo puzzles using pictures that represent a number. Students present pictures to the class to see if they can guess the number the picture represents. For example, the number twenty three could be represented by a picture of Michael Jordan. The harder to figure out, the better! With these numbers, you can launch all types of activities (graph, perform functions, etc.)

GOAL: TO EDIT AND ENHANCE DIGITAL PHOTOS IN CREATIVE AND FUN WAYS.

OVERVIEW

Online photo editors allow users to upload photos and enhance them in many ways without needing to load a piece of software onto a computer. You can perform common tasks such as cropping, resizing, and removing red eye. However, in addition to this, you and your students can also add text, stickers, animations, borders, and many other effects.

Most photo editors also work in conjunction with photo sharing sites, such as Facebook, MySpace, Flickr, Twitter, Photobucket, and Webshots. This means you can work with images in both directions. For example, you can pull pictures *from* these sites as well as upload enhanced images *to* your accounts on these sites. These image editors also make it easy to e-mail photos, save files to your computer, and print as well.

Once you and your students are finished with editing pictures, they can be saved and utilized with many of the other tools in this book. Photos are essential elements of digital storytelling, Prezi presentations, VoiceThreads, Glogs, timeline creators, and many other potential technology projects. Your students will *love* being able to edit their photos, either as a stand-alone activity or to be used within a larger project!

BUT FIRST...

→ These tools require the latest version of Adobe Flash, so be sure to download this on any student or teacher computer before attempting to use for instruction.

GETTING STARTED

There are multiple image editors to choose from, and they all work relatively the same way. Here are a few that you might want to check out to get the best fit for your needs. They are ranked based on my personal preference:

1. Picnik: **www.picnik.com**
2. Aviary: **www.aviary.com**
3. FotoFlexer: **www.fotoflexer.com**
4. Lunapic: **www.lunapic.com**
5. Pixenate: **www.pixenate.com**

The first step in getting started with these tools is to upload a picture. Find the "upload image" or "upload picture" button, locate the picture you would like to edit, and upload it to the editor. Once the picture is loaded, it takes you straight to the photo-editing window of the site.

Now it's time to start the editing process! There will be several ways to edit pictures available to you. Here are some terms that you will encounter within the editing process that might be unfamiliar to you:

Auto Fix/Enhance: This tool will attempt to automatically improve the photo; for example, enhancing the colors to be more vibrant.

Brightness: This tool essentially makes the photo darker or lighter.

Contrast: This tool boosts or lessens color intensity by adjusting the level of gray scale in a photo.

Crop: This tool allows you to discard parts of the photo you don't want. Select the part of the photo you'd like to zoom in on, and press "crop"–the rest of the photo will disappear.

Effects: This tool changes the entire picture in different ways—turning it black and white or twisting the image, for example.

Red Eye: This tool removes red eye from photos. After selecting it, try zooming in and clicking on the subject's pupils.

Rotate: This tool rotates the picture, often in 90 degree increments.

To apply an edit, simply click the tool you would like to try and start editing. There may also be an "Apply" button that you need to hit between edits. But don't worry—if you make a change you are unhappy with, you can hit the "Undo/Cancel" button or simply press "Back" on your browser and reload the original picture.

Finally, when the picture looks the way you envision, it is time to save, publish, or share it. If you want to publish the picture to social media sites, most photo editors have buttons for Facebook, MySpace, Flickr, etc., so you can share photos directly through those services. Click the "E-mail" button to share the picture via e-mail with friends, family, or your students.

USE IN THE CLASSROOM

Photo editing is a natural activity for students in the Net Generation; they love to express themselves in this way. Taking a picture and customizing it to make it their own creation is a powerful way to activate student learning. Editing a photo can also be used as a strategy within a larger project. If creating a digital story about the Great Depression, for example, you may have students upload and "age" a picture with effects such as sepia to make it look as if it came from the 1930s.

OTHER ISSUES TO CONSIDER

→ As you explore these image editors, you will undoubtedly notice that some of the features are premium-content only. Most of the common editing features discussed in this book are free, however.

→ Image files that your students are working with can be stored on your school's network folder.

→ If utilizing this digital tool as a piece of a larger project, make sure students don't get bogged down in the photo-editing process; they will spend hours on this if you let them, which might have a negative impact on the project as a whole.

→ Here are some royalty free sites where you can download photographs. However, be aware that each site has its own guidelines for use that you must adhere to:

1. Flickr Creative Commons (**www.flickr.com/creativecommons**)
2. FreeDigitalPhotos.net (**www.freedigitalphotos.net**)
3. Stock.XCHNG (**www.sxc.hu**)

CONTENT AREA TIE-INS

Science

→ Assign groups and give each a different topic (if studying extreme weather, these could be tornadoes, hurricanes, hailstorms, and blizzards, for example). Each group then researches and uploads photos that represent this topic and adds text boxes to each with facts about the image.

→ Have students upload photos that show the life cycle of an animal and label each stage by using the text box feature.

→ Upload a scientific diagram (e.g. parts of a plant) with blanks and have students add text boxes to fill in the blanks.

Social Studies

→ Have students locate and download images of monuments or landmarks located in the county under study. Once uploaded to the image editor, have students add graphics that point out key elements or text boxes that describe where the monument is located and why it is important.

→ Have students find photos of historical figures and add speech bubbles of things they might say in the present day. Have fun with this one!

→ Give students several pictures of money from different regions of the world they have studied and ask them to figure out where the money comes from and add a caption of the country's name to the picture.

LIVE INTERNET VIDEO STREAMING

Language Arts

→ Invite an author into your school for students to interview.

→ Host weekly (or monthly, depending on time) book chats, where students can log in and discuss a book they're reading with you.

→ Host a regularly scheduled show where your students read their writing and broadcast it to the world.

Math

→ Host a weekly Homework Helper from your home at night: thirty to forty minutes where you make yourself available to your students and their parents to answer any questions they may have.

→ Ask students to produce and broadcast a quarterly show to review topics that may be on their quarterly test. Record the show and embed it on your website so students can watch it at home to help prepare.

GOAL: TO STREAM LIVE VIDEO OVER THE INTERNET THAT IS OPEN TO PUBLIC VIEWING.

OVERVIEW

Live Internet video streaming refers to the practice of broadcasting live via the Internet using a webcam and microphone. By far, the most popular way to utilize this strategy is through Ustream, located at **www.ustream.tv**.

Ustream was founded in 2006 as a way to help soldiers overseas connect with their loved ones back home. Since then, it has evolved to cover all sorts of unforeseen territory. Ustream users from all over the world now broadcast their daily lives, soccer matches, video games, and even their pets!

The amazing part is how quickly and easily you can set up a live stream. It is very simple to set up a live stream that others can hop onto, view, and discuss via live chat.

BUT FIRST...

→ You will need a working webcam hooked up to your computer to utilize this tool.

→ Before going live to the Internet, contact your IT department to find out your school's policies regarding broadcasting students. You may need to obtain parental permission before broadcasting.

GETTING STARTED

The first thing to do is sign up for a Ustream account. Once you are logged in, make sure your webcam is hooked up and functioning and then click on the "Broadcast Now" button. From here, give your show a name, a category, and a description of the show's content. Now you are ready to go live. After clicking the "Broadcast" button, you will see the broadcasting box with your smiling face (or whatever your camera is pointed at). You are now broadcasting to the world. All viewers have to do is go to the unique URL that is provided by Ustream and they will see live video and hear live audio.

Once you are broadcasting live, you will want to see how it appears to others logging into Ustream. Hop onto another computer and search for your broadcast. Search for it from the Ustream Web page by entering the title of your show into the search bar. When you see it come up in the search results, click it to view the live feed.

While you have both screens up, play with the audio and video quality settings to achieve the overall look and sound you want. There is a two-to-three second delay with the broadcast, and the quality of the video stream will depend greatly on a few variables: the quality of your webcam, the Internet connection, the computer running the webcam, and the computer viewing the webcam. The better the quality of each, the better the live stream will appear.

Other Ustream tools you will want to experiment with include:

→ Live chat: This feature allows the broadcaster and the audience members to interact while the show is being streamed.

→ Poll: This feature allows you to ask questions of your audience, to which they can respond (with responses updating live).

→ Text & Videos: This feature allows you to add text layers onto your live stream.

→ Start Record: This feature allows you to record the session. When the session is over, click "Stop Record" and save the file to your Ustream account for later viewing.

USE IN THE CLASSROOM

Live Internet broadcasting can be a great publishing tool. Providing an arena for students to create and host regularly scheduled, live Internet productions makes learning meaningful and engaging. Broadcasts can also be used to report on live events such as field trips, class demonstrations, or local happenings.

Finally, Ustream can be used in many ways to enhance communication with parents and the surrounding community, sharing the great things happening in your class or school. Parents can even tune into live shows you stream during the day.

OTHER ISSUES TO CONSIDER

→ You can password-protect your show so that only those with a password can watch. When logged into Ustream, click the "Manage Your Show" link on the left and click "Settings." At the top, you'll see the option to make your show private and a place to add a password. You can also manage whether or not comments are moderated—or even allowed at all.

→ You need to play around with video quality and frame rates because these can have dramatic effects on how the broadcast looks to your viewers.

→ Networking with Twitter, MySpace, and Facebook is possible on Ustream, which allows you interact with others from both sites while streaming live. Because you are also able to quickly and easily share the link via these sites, your friends or followers can view your show.

→ Caution: Some streams can be explicit because Ustream has no filters. Don't allow students free reign to search the site.

→ Make sure to record shows so you can archive them for later use or rebroadcasting.

→ Backgrounds, logos, etc., allow you to customize the look/feel of each show. When setting up your show, click on the "Design" tab to try some out.

→ The site's Mobile app, Ustream Live Broadcaster, allows users to stream live video, with sound, straight from their iPhone, Android, or Nokia devices. It is incredibly easy to use, and it links directly to your Ustream account. Expect other phones to offer this same functionality soon. Broadcasting instantly to the Internet from anywhere can have powerful educational uses. Visit **www.ustream.tv/mobile** to download this app.

CONTENT AREA TIE-INS

Science

→ Find live animal cams on Ustream by browsing through the "Animals" category. Your student can watch eagles in their nests, dogs taking care of their young, and even an alpaca farm.

→ Invite students to host a weekly or monthly show where they perform experiments at home. Friends can get together and record themselves doing an experiment for the world to see.

→ Broadcast and record experiments that you perform in your classroom. Combine this with ePals (found on p. 48) to conduct joint experiments across the globe.

Social Studies

→ Broadcast live from a field trip. You can use a wireless laptop or smartphone anywhere there is an Internet connection. Invite students to broadcast back home to their parents, who can follow along and check their progress.

→ Head to an important town hall or school board meeting and broadcast the event. Discuss with students the protocol and procedures for passing laws or making new policies.

TOOL #12

MESSAGE BOARDS

CONTENT AREA TIE-INS

Language Arts

→ Start a word association thread by posting a word or phrase and instructing students to log in and post the very first thing that comes to their mind upon seeing the previous post. Let this thread play out and talk about how words trigger certain emotions and feelings in the reader.

→ Build a character by starting a thread whose title is simply a name. The next poster adds one attribute to the character and each poster thereafter builds from what was previously said. Attributes can deal with the character's personality, physical description, or background. Watch the character evolve in front of your eyes!

→ Start a "whisper down the lane" story, where you contribute the first sentence and ask each successive poster to write the next sentence in the story. At the end, discuss how the story evolved and whether or not it made sense.

Science

→ Identify forums that pertain to your topic, then have your students participate, asking questions of the experts that contribute to that message board.

→ Start a latitude/longitude quiz thread by posting coordinates for a recognizable object (your school, a monument, etc.) The next poster identifies the object, and then posts a new set of coordinates. The next poster then finds this object and post their own, and so on. Coordinates are easily obtained within Google Earth (found on p. 54).

→ Ask students and their parents to respond in a thread about their "green" habits at home: how they make their home more energy-efficient, what they recycle (if anything), etc.

OVERVIEW

Message boards (also called Internet forums) have been areas for discussion on the Web since the mid-1990s (an eternity in the world of the Internet!) Each board typically focuses on a shared interest, such as a video game, favorite football team, celebrities, and many other topics. So many boards exist, in fact, that you would be hard-pressed to find a topic that did *not* have some sort of discussion about it somewhere on the Internet.

Forums are places where users can register (most times, anonymously) and add their own opinions about the topic at hand. Forums are usually sorted into different areas to keep discussions focused (for example, you could separate discussions based on the chapters of a book you are studying or different units your class is working through). Each user can either start or contribute to an individual discussion, called a thread. Within this thread, one can offer their own ideas as well as reply to specific thoughts posted by others in the thread. In this way, discussions can evolve rapidly and points/counterpoints flow freely.

Most message boards are controlled by the creator and a moderator. Think of a moderator in the same way you would a referee or a debate mediator. The moderator's job is to enforce the rules of the message board. For example, if one of the rules is that profanity is not allowed, a moderator has the power to delete posts and suspend or ban users that use obscenities.

BUT FIRST...

→ Remember to check your county's policies on online interaction with students before you begin utilizing message boards.

GETTING STARTED

There are many options to create message boards. The first place to look is in your school's own website structure. You may already have the option to create a message board on your pre-established class or school page. If this is not an option or if your school's website is difficult to manage, other sites that allow you to create message boards are ProBoards (**www.proboards. com**), boards2go.com (**www.boards2go.com**), or Aimoo (**www.aimoo. com**). You can also create message boards within Ning (featured on p. 66 of this book).

Wherever the forum resides, the basic setup procedures are essentially the same. You will need a title for your forum and some broad categories for discussion. For example, in a science class, these categories could consist of curriculum strands, such as planets, weather, animal adaptations, etc. After you have set up your forum categories, you will need to set up how you want your users to contribute to the forum. With most message boards, you have complete power over what can or cannot be posted—images, video, text, audio, other files, etc. It is important to think about what you want to do with your forums when you set them up so users have the freedom to create your vision. For example, if you plan to use the message board to have students post pictures of something they've researched, make sure you allow users to post pictures.

Once you are all set up, you are ready to start your first thread. Many message boards have an introductory thread where users post a little about themselves. This is a good way to get students involved with the message board initially.

USE IN THE CLASSROOM

Anytime you can encourage thoughtful, focused discussion, you will see benefits for your students. Message boards allow you to do just that—create a structured environment where students can post their own thoughts, ideas, and feelings as well as reply to other people's posts (including yours). There are many opportunities for give and take within the message board format, and you may find that some of your quieter students really grab hold of this medium to express their thoughts. There is also a comfort factor involved, in that students can flesh out their ideas in their own environment, free from the pressure of speaking up in class.

Message boards can be utilized not only as a communication tool for your class, but also as a research tool. As stated above, there are thousands of message boards already out there discussing a multitude of topics; I challenge you to do an Internet search for "[insert topic here] message board" and see what you find! It is important to remember that, when using the Internet, you are most likely not the first person to ask a certain question. Simply entering a question into a search engine will often point to pages upon pages of results of that same question appearing on various message boards. Answers to these questions can therefore be found or pieced together through careful searching.

Lastly, the message board you create will only be as effective as you make it! If you are not a regular contributor, your students will not be either. To make your message board a success, you are a crucial ingredient in encouraging relevant discussion and moderating debate.

OTHER ISSUES TO CONSIDER

→ Be careful about allowing students to rely on message boards for research. Many boards will be blocked at school, but the ones that are accessible can be difficult for filters to scan for inappropriate material. If some such material gets though, use it as a teachable moment about utilizing the Internet for research in general.

→ Instruct your students to avoid "me, too" posts: posts in which all they contribute is a sentence or two stating their agreement with one of the previous posters. Encourage students to define what they agree with and to develop their own points of view.

→ When visiting a message board, first be a "lurker"—someone who does not sign up but "lurks" in the shadows to learn the written and unwritten rules of that message board. Because each message board is a community, it has its own style. Make sure it is a match for you and your students before you participate.

→ Many message boards with unsuitable content for schoolwork can bypass your school's Web filter, so don't encourage students to search for message boards on a topic. Instead, find some on your own that apply, and restrict message board activity to approved sites.

Math

→ Create forum categories for each major curriculum strand and encourage students to lean on their peers (and you) when they get stuck on a certain type of problem. Message boards are a great place for students to discuss strategies they tried that did not work.

→ Pose a difficult problem of the week and give extra credit to the first student to post the answer along with their work.

→ Utilize the Number-Picture Thread, a common message board thread. The original poster (you) posts a picture that somehow represents the number one (for example, a picture from the first Star Wars movie, or a football player wearing a number one jersey). Each poster thereafter follows the trend with the next number in the sequence (picture for two, followed by a picture for three, etc.) Start this thread and watch how creative your students get.

Social Studies

→ Pose difficult current events topics and ask students to take a stance and post arguments that support their stance.

→ Create usernames of important figures you are studying, and hand them out to students. Students log on and contribute posts as these historical figures. If you want to have even more fun with this idea, keep the student identities secret, and see if they can guess when the discussion is over.

MIND MAPPING

CONTENT AREA TIE-INS

Language Arts

→ Have students create a tree diagram that shows the problem, solution, setting, and characters within a story they have read or written themselves.

→ Ask students to create a flow map that plans out an upcoming writing assignment.

→ Use a compare/contrast map to evaluate two characters, genres, novels, etc.

Math

→ Have students create flowcharts that show the steps in the process of solving a word problem.

→ Use a tree diagram to classify concepts such as geometric shapes or types of fractions, numbers, and triangles, etc.

→ Ask students to create a floor plan of the classroom, complete with area, perimeter, scaling information, and measurements of objects within the room.

GOAL: STUDENTS CREATE INTERACTIVE GRAPHIC ORGANIZERS INDIVIDUALLY OR IN COLLABORATIVE GROUPS.

OVERVIEW

Mind maps are powerful tools that help students organize their thoughts. Traditional mind maps, also called graphic organizers, have been used in classrooms for many years in the form of Venn diagrams, bubble maps, flow maps, and maps for organizing the writing process. The Web-based mind-mapping tools have taken the traditional pencil and paper version and made some significant improvements. Not only do the shapes and text look much neater (for messy artists such as myself), but a key feature encourages the core skill of collaboration. Online mind maps allow multiple students to work on maps together so that multiple users can brainstorm and "think about thinking" together. Because the software keeps a copy of all previous, saved versions, invited users can view and edit the diagrams without altering prior work. This makes for a safe, easy, and collaborative environment.

BUT FIRST...

→ These tools utilize Adobe Flash, so be sure to have the latest version on each computer you are using.

GETTING STARTED

Mind mapping tools feature several excellent options, and they all function in roughly the same manner. My top three choices are Webspiration (**www.mywebspiration.com**), Gliffy (**www.gliffy.com**), and Bubbl.us (**www.bubbl.us**). The main differences between them are relatively cosmetic: Webspiration offers the most images and shapes to customize your diagram; Gliffy has a medium amount; Bubbl.us offers little variety in this area. Since they are all free, I encourage you to view examples of each (or register and try all three), before choosing which one you'd like to use with your students.

After registering and logging in, the process of creating maps is straightforward within all of these tools. You choose from alternative shapes and link them with arrows, lines, or whatever way you like. In this way, you can put a topic in the middle and brainstorm links, make a flowchart, create a tree diagram for categorization, or create any other type of map you or your students can imagine. The interface is "drag and drop,"which leads to a very intuitive experience.

Along the way, each map can be customized to fit your needs; you can color-code boxes, change box shapes or line thickness, or even import your own images for use within the map.

At any step in this process, you can add collaborators to work on the map with you. This is done by clicking on "Share" or "Sharing." You will be asked to add users, and the software will send them e-mails inviting them to view or edit the document depending on the rights given in the invitation. Finally, you can print these maps for an offline copy to display or keep in a student portfolio.

USE IN THE CLASSROOM

Across all subject levels, mind-mapping graphic organizers promote thinking skills, such as brainstorming, classification, cause-effect, sequencing, compare/contrast, and part-whole relationships. Any opportunity you have to give students a chance to organize their thinking pays big benefits. For some students, the use of graphic organizers can be a critical component of classroom success.

The collaborative aspect of these tools makes them stand out even more. Any two users can work together on the same graphic organizer wherever there is an Internet connection. Even better, there is no need to install a program on your computer – these tools are housed entirely online. Add in the ease of use and the ability to print and export files, and you have an excellent tool to use with students on a regular basis.

OTHER ISSUES TO CONSIDER

→ In Gliffy, you may only load images that are 1 MB or less, so no huge images.

→ Gliffy is the only option of the three that allows you to export your map as a JPEG. The others require you to use the screen-shot function on your computer.

→ Webspiration was developed by Inspiration Software, Inc. and so looks similar to their Inspiration program. If you or your students have used Inspiration software before, Webspiration might be the easiest Web-based tool to transition to.

→ An upgrade to the premium Gliffy version gives you a free version of the tool, as well as the ability to manage users and folders. You can try the pro version for thirty days to see if it suits you better. If you go premium, pricing is 50 percent off for educators!

→ Another new tool in this realm is SpicyNodes, which is located at **www.spicynodes.org**. This tool was in a beta form at the time of this writing, but it's worth keeping an eye on.

As part of our study of the Japanese samurai and their code of honor (bushido), students used SpicyNodes, a mind-mapping website, to create a map of their own virtues. After students had finished their writing, they created a node map, with each virtue represented as a node... SpicyNodes allowed students to customize the way their writing was presented, and this resulted in a creation that was easily embeddable in each student's blog.

MEREDITH STEWART
Language Arts & Social Studies

CONTENT AREA TIE-INS

Science

→ Create cause-effect diagrams that show outcomes of an experiment performed in class.

→ Utilize a compare/contrast diagram to reveal the similarities and differences between two concepts or objects being studied (animal species, types of rock, landforms, etc.)

→ Have students create a part/whole chart that shows the parts of a plant, the layers of the Earth, or any other pertinent topic.

Social Studies

→ Use a descriptive bubble chart to share a current event, an important figure, or attributes of a country, etc.

→ Allow students to create a flowchart of events that led to a significant moment in history.

→ Use cause/effect maps to study inventions and their impacts on society.

TOOL #14

NING

OVERVIEW

Ning allows you to create your own social network for your classes. It functions similarly to Facebook and MySpace, as each user gets his or her own fully customizable page/space. The advantage of using Ning in schools is that you have complete control over all content. You can set it up so that you must approve all users and photos/videos that are uploaded, and you can delete anything under your Ning's umbrella. This makes for an easy-to-use networking site that maintains the positive aspects of social networking while severely limiting the negative.

BUT FIRST...

→ Many schools have policies regarding social networking that involves teachers and students. Be sure to contact your IT department or administrative team to get clarification on these policies so you are protected while using this tool with students.

→ Students will need e-mail addresses to participate.

GETTING STARTED

Starting a Ning for your classroom or school could not be easier. While Ning recently decided to start charging for its basic service, a loophole still allows educators to create free sites. Pearson graciously offered to sponsor free educator Nings, but the link to sign up for this service is hidden on the regular site. To get started, go to **www.about.ning.com/pearsonsponsorship**. This URL takes you to an application form to sign up for your own free Ning. Fill out the application, submit it, and await word of acceptance in your e-mail—along with instructions for setting up your site.

Once your Ning is approved, the first thing you will want to do is determine its purpose. When thinking about what features to add, try to envision how you will utilize them for learning tasks. Ask yourself questions such as: "Will I have my students post in a message board/forum?" "Will my students need to post video?" "How much time do I have to approve all videos/photos?"

I encourage you to start simple and work your way up to some of the more advanced features. Don't overload your Ning at the very beginning (this can overwhelm not only you, but also your students and parents).

Next, you'll customize the pages with templates that change colors and contours with just a few clicks. You can further tailor the pages by adding images to the header, side, or within the body of the site. These could be your school's mascot or some other representative image.

Once you have the features set and have customized how you want it to look, take some time to play around with each of the features you have selected. Upload some photos, upload video, customize your individual page, post a test blog and a test forum topic, etc. All of these tests can be deleted before you go "live."

Once you feel comfortable with your Ning, it is time to put it to the test by inviting users. To do this, simply click "Invite members." This will allow you to send invitations out to e-mail addresses. Once the invitations are sent out, users will begin to register. They should also customize their own pages and

---

CONTENT AREA TIE-INS

Language Arts

→ Encourage students to post book reports as blogs.

→ Start forum discussions that talk about a novel you are studying.

→ Have students post persuasive arguments as blog posts. Critique the style and substance, and guide discussions toward productive outcomes.

Math

→ Find math videos on TeacherTube (**www.teachertube.com**) or SchoolTube (**www.schooltube.com**) and post them to your Ning.

→ Record screen casts of how to solve problems (see screencasting tool on p. 74 of this book) and post them to the Ning.

→ Ask students to take pictures of geometric concepts under study to post to the Ning.

start to "friend" one another (students will be able to do this quickly and intuitively). Once users are in, you are ready to use the Ning for learning opportunities in the classroom.

USE IN THE CLASSROOM

Your students are going to love you for starting your own class social networking site! Sites similar to this are their primary mode of communication at home every day, and they will take to it quickly. Ning offers opportunities for writing and critical thinking through blog and forum posts, as well as the ability to collaborate on projects by uploading pictures and video and adding comments to each. There is also a calendar feature that will allow you to post important dates for students to remember. The amount of communication that will flow through this tool will sell you on it quite quickly.

OTHER ISSUES TO CONSIDER

→ Remember to always maintain professionalism when interacting with students online.

→ Sometimes, it could be appropriate to invite parents to your Ning. Just keep in mind that students may feel that their freedom of expression is limited when their mom or dad is poking around the same site.

→ Focus on an environment of mutual respect where all opinions and points of view are appreciated. Encourage respectful debate and eliminate drama wherever possible.

→ Remember to encourage students to cite sources for any photos or videos that they bring into the Ning.

→ Ning is also a fantastic place to network with other educators. Two good starting sites are The Educator's PLN (**www.edupln.ning.com**) and Classroom 2.0 (**www.classroom20.com**). The former is a smaller place for educators to build their personal learning networks, and the latter is a large environment where members discuss and reflect about the art of teaching.

The assignment was for students to write letters to their US senators on an issue that interested them. I created a Ning with discussions for the major issues that were discussed on the websites of the two senators. The students went to the websites and posted what they learned about the issues that they were interested in. They read each other's posts and added to them, creating a rich collaborative environment.

HADLEY FERGUSON
History

CONTENT AREA TIE-INS

Science

→ Have students generate and respond to forum topics that debate the topic at hand. For example, if studying bacteria, the debating forum posts could be "Bacteria rules!" and "Bacteria is our enemy!" Students post ideas to support each argument.

→ Have students research and post photos or video that illustrate a scientific concept (for example, tornado pictures/video if studying extreme weather or solar panels/windmill farms if studying green energy).

→ Create a poll using the application Polldaddy. This is a free, embeddable gadget that you can place on your Ning. Use it to poll students about what type of experiment they would like to try next, their attitudes about dissection, their opinions about their previous test, etc.)

Social Studies

→ Post a provocative question linked to current events to elicit personal responses.

→ Schedule a chat session with a congressional representative and invite them to your Ning to share thoughts and ideas.

→ Have students research primary source material and post it with a description of where it comes from and how it relates to the topic.

PODCASTING

Language Arts

→ Have students interview a person using an MP3 player. Questions should be carefully planned. Use the recording as a springboard for writing.

→ Allow students to use MP3 players to read their own writing into the microphone. After recording, students listen to themselves reading their work and make appropriate revisions.

→ Interview students about what they are seeing or hearing during multi-day field trips. Post these files each night so that parents at home can follow along with their child's trip.

Math

→ Let students take turns describing a shape into the microphone, while others listen to the description and try to draw it. Depending on the outcomes, discuss what made the explanation easy or difficult to follow, and guide students toward a greater understanding of the shape.

→ Have students take MP3 players home to interview their parents about their attitudes about math, both now and when they were in school. Listen to the interviews and discuss how feelings about math affects performance and perception.

GOAL: TO RECORD AND PRODUCE AN AUDIO RECORDING RELATED TO A LEARNING TASK.

OVERVIEW

The word "podcasting" was cleverly created by merging "broadcasting" with a shortened version of the word "iPod." As its name implies, podcasting refers to the idea of using an MP3 player, iPod, or even a microphone attached to a computer to record audio, which is then published via iTunes or through similar venues on the Internet. You can publish a regularly occurring podcast (think of it as a daily or weekly radio show), or a stand-alone recording. It's also good to note that while the term "podcasting" originated as a form of publication—and I encourage you to publish to the Internet whenever possible—it has evolved in schools to refer to any type of digital audio recording.

BUT FIRST...

→ When purchasing MP3 players for classroom use, make sure they come equipped with microphones; or, if using iPods, that you order attachable microphones.

→ Podcasting can also be done with any type of digital voice recorder—just make sure you buy one with USB capability.

GETTING STARTED

The very first step in the podcasting process is choosing how you want to record audio. There are a couple of options: using a MP3 player or your computer. Remember that, in general, you get what you pay for. A cheaper MP3 player will typically have shorter battery life or may not be rugged enough for heavy student use. On the other hand, since your primary purpose for the device is simple recording, a high-end device does not make sense either. The best strategy is to buy a player that gets good reviews for battery life and wear and tear but does not break the bank on a tight school budget.

Whatever you buy should have a built-in microphone, above all else. Note that not all MP3 players do. Another option is to use a microphone with a computer. Many laptops have built-in microphones; desktop models usually don't. One very significant drawback to choosing a computer/mic setup is that this option tethers you and your students to a computer.

Once you have chosen a recording device, figure out how it records files. Some have simple record buttons; others may require you to dig through menus to record. After that, the rest falls into place. Start recording and speak clearly into the microphone. After recording, you will need to transfer the audio to your computer if you are using MP3 files. This involves connecting the device via a USB cord, finding the audio files, and copying them to your computer. At this time, you can also listen to your files, edit, and rename them as needed.

If this seems overwhelming, here are a few beginners' guides that I recommend:

→ "Beginner's Guide to Podcast Creation" by Kirk McElhearn: **www.ilounge.com/index.php/articles/comments/ beginners-guide-to-podcast-creation**

→ "Podcast Essentials: A Beginner's Guide to Producing a Podcast" by The Phantom Blot: **www.hubpages.com/hub/ Podcast-Essentials-A-Beginners-Guide-to-Producing-a-Podcast**

→ Podcasting and Podcatching for the Absolute Beginner on Wikispaces: **www.podcastingforbeginners.wikispaces.com**

Finally, it is time to publish! To understand podcast publishing better, it is helpful to separate them into two separate groups: regularly released and stand-alone. A regularly released podcast is like a weekly radio show. Listeners will expect to see a new podcast put up at a regularly scheduled time. In contrast, a stand-alone podcast exists on its own.

Both types can be published by uploading them to your school website and providing a link. They can also be sent out via e-mail (although, if the recording is long, file size may be an issue). Regularly released podcasts can be published through iTunes or simply updated on an alternative hosting website. Three good, free options for hosting your podcasts are Podbean.com (**www.podbean.com**), PodOmatic (**www.podomatic.com**), and MyPodcast. com (**www.mypodcast.com**).

USE IN THE CLASSROOM

Podcasting requires careful planning to reach its full effectiveness. As a teacher, you need to plan the questions you are going to ask students. You also have to prepare students to respond by letting them know what to expect before hitting the record button. Students also need to do some planning by laying out their thoughts and collecting themselves before recording. A successful podcast is clear and easy to understand, which can take some practice.

Podcasting is also an excellent tool for teachers. It can be used as a way to communicate regularly with parents about class events and student expectations. If you post this information weekly to your website via podcast, parents are better informed and more likely to become active participants in their child's learning. The uses of podcasting in the classroom are limited only by one's imagination.

OTHER ISSUES TO CONSIDER

→ MP3 players that use rechargeable batteries often have battery issues, so I recommend having enough batteries on hand to completely replace an entire set. If your MP3 players recharge through a computer connection, and you have less computers than MP3 players, consider purchasing USB hubs.

→ Make sure you are following your school or district guidelines about recording students or classes.

→ Standard iPods do not have microphones built into them, so you will need to order separate microphones to record with them.

→ Always name audio files very descriptively and place them into distinct folders so you can avoid listening to each file to know its contents.

→ You can edit sound files easily with one of two easy-to-use, free programs: Audacity (**www.audacity.sourceforge.net**) and Goldwave (**www.goldwave.com**). These programs allow you to edit parts out, enhance volume, save as different file types, etc.

CONTENT AREA TIE-INS

Science

→ Have students create instructions on how to conduct an experiment. Record these instructions as a podcast, and assign a group to attempt to create the experiment using the instructions. Talk to students about the importance of clarity and explicit instructions when conducting experiments and how this affects the outcome.

→ Allow students to record a weekly podcast that defines the science terms they have worked on that week.

→ Let students give their impressions of what they are seeing, smelling, hearing, touching, or tasting while actively doing projects or collecting data in the field.

Social Studies

→ Find out if there is anyone in your community who comes from or has visited the region of the world you are studying. Create interview questions and allow students to conduct interviews using MP3 players.

→ Have students record older relatives reflecting about life during their youth. Oral history is a strong part of our cultural past.

PREZI

Language Arts

→ Create a presentation about the major plot points of the novel you are working with.

→ Have students create a Prezi about the steps of the writing/revision process.

→ Ask students to use a Prezi presentation to illustrate the similarities and differences between books, authors, poets, settings, genres, etc.

→ Let students create a mind map to describe a character they have written a story about.

Math

→ Illustrate the steps in a geometry proof by scanning/inserting pictures and having students create each information section as a step in the process.

→ Have students create a presentation about the steps in the process of solving word problems.

→ Have students create a simple Prezi with numbers in a patterned sequence. Viewers of the presentation are asked to decipher the pattern.

GOAL: TO CREATE A VISUALLY DISTINCTIVE, INTERACTIVE PRESENTATION.

OVERVIEW

Prezi is a radically new way of thinking about traditional presentations. It allows you to do the normal things you expect, like adding text, images, video, etc., but it executes them in exciting formats. Think of your presentation as a giant, three-dimensional map of information separated into scattered sections. Prezi allows you to create these sections of information at different angles and "zooms" from section to section.

In other words, instead of clicking from slide to slide like a traditional presentation, in Prezi you'll zoom from section to section as you present content. The effect is a sharp-looking presentation that will make your audience sit up and take notice.

BUT FIRST...

→ Prezi works best in your browser with the latest version of Adobe Flash. Prezi also recommends the Safari or Mozilla Firefox browsers for greatest compatibility.

GETTING STARTED

Register with Prezi first at **www.prezi.com**. For teachers, Prezi has begun to offer educator accounts with additional benefits over a traditional free account. From the main Prezi page, click "Sign up" and then select the "Student/ Teacher Licenses" button. This type of registration allows educators much more storage, removes the watermark, and allows you to make a Prezi private.

Instead of playing around with the Prezi features, I recommend that you view the tutorial on the homepage first. Prezi is different from any digital tool you have experienced. The functionality can be difficult to grasp at first because of the way it defines how to create a presentation slideshow.

After viewing the tutorial, go ahead and create your first Prezi, starting with the information sections. The spoked wheel at the upper left side of the presentation helps you add objects. Each circle you click expands the wheel and offers spokes that provide options, such as adding lines, frames, text, colors, paths, or media. As you click each of these circles, more options for placement are given. Explore these options to see how Prezi functions.

The best way to go about making a Prezi is to group information into places on the 3-D map. After you finish one section of information, zoom out with your mouse wheel and find another spot on the Prezi map to post information. Repeat the steps above until you have two or more areas of information.

Next, link these sections together by creating a path. A path is simply the order in which you wish your information be displayed. This will sequence your presentation. Finally, to view your Prezi, click on "Show." Now you can zoom between sections by using the arrow buttons as well as viewing the presentation in full-screen mode.

Once your presentation is to your liking, it is hosted on the Internet. To share with others or view it yourself, you can simply copy and paste the link that is provided. If you are presenting in an area that does not have an Internet connection, Prezi also allows you to download and print the presentation.

USE IN THE CLASSROOM

A new presentation method always grabs attention! Using Prezi is an excellent way to get your class excited about creating presentations again. It definitely solves the collective "Not another PowerPoint" groan that you hear from students everywhere.

In addition to the novelty factor, Prezi is a tool that your spatial learners will love! It is visually stunning, and it allows spatial learners a chance to really shine in the classroom. Furthermore, Prezi can have a large impact on any activity that involves sequencing. The steps in the presentation can each represent steps in a process, truly bringing them to life.

OTHER ISSUES TO CONSIDER

→ Take the tour, and then retake the Prezi homepage tour. Note the "Learn" tab on your Prezi account; it offers presentations on some of the tool's more innovative tricks.

→ Prezi automatically saves your changes as you go, so you won't have to worry about losing any information if you accidentally close the window.

→ Prezi also allows you to invite others to edit/collaborate on your presentation. When logged into Prezi, click "Share," and you will have the ability to add e-mails for invitations. You can also create groups of e-mails so you can share future presentations more easily, like a "Students" group, for example.

→ When sharing your Prezi, you can allow it to be public as well as allow it to be reused by others. This means that you will be opening up the presentation so that people can copy it, alter it however they want, and use it for their own purposes.

→ Many Prezi presentations are waiting for reuse. Why make your own if there is already a good one out there? Use the search box to find them.

→ Downloading a Prezi presentation is not simple for newbie users. What actually downloads when you hit "download" is a zip file that contains everything you need to take with you. To get the presentation to work, you need to extract these files. After files are extracted, you will see a "prezi.exe" icon. Double-click this icon to start your presentation (remember, you'll need the latest version of Adobe Flash to play it).

CONTENT AREA TIE-INS

Science

→ Create a presentation about the life stages of certain plants or animals.

→ Let students create a presentation about cause and effect in the science world. For example, global temperatures rising would become the first info section and the next gives reasons for this occurrence.

Social Studies

→ Create a sequenced presentation, such as a timeline of historical events, with each info section representing a new event on the timeline.

→ Ask students to create a presentation for the local school board to lobby for something your class or schools needs. Local school board members will be astonished by your presentation methods!

→ Use Prezi to develop a biography about a famous figure. Each information section could depict a stage of that person's life.

TOOL #17

SCHOOLTUBE

CONTENT AREA TIE-INS

Language Arts

→ Have students dress up as different characters from a novel and then be "interviewed." This could take the format of a talk show or regular broadcasting-style interview.

→ Seek out local authors and have students conduct interviews asking about the way they write and how they come up with and formulate stories.

→ Talk about the quality of dialogue in your students' stories by asking them to record themselves reading the dialogue they've written and then determine if it sounds "real." Discuss how to create meaningful dialogue in stories.

Math

→ Have students create a word problem and then act it out to find the solution.

→ Create math characters with the students to use in funny videos (Captain Isosceles versus the Scalene Screamer... RatioMan and his sidekick, Proportion Boy).

→ Ask students to conduct live interviews/ challenges with their friends, family, and other teachers in the building; they prepare a math problem and put people on the spot to see if they can solve it!

→ Encourage the student who is the best in the class at solving a certain type of problem to create a video on his or her method and post it for the rest of the class to watch if they get stuck.

OVERVIEW

Think of SchoolTube (**www.schooltube.com**) as YouTube for students and teachers. Like YouTube, SchoolTube allows you to create channels that group videos together so they are easier to locate. It provides many of the same features that have made YouTube explosively popular, such as the ability to upload, rate, and comment upon videos.

The large and significant difference between the two services is that SchoolTube videos are moderated and approved by educators like you and me before they are posted publicly. This keeps SchoolTube safe while still allowing students a lot of freedom in the types of videos they submit.

BUT FIRST...

→ Browse through the videos on SchoolTube to get an idea of what is out there. This may spark some ideas for your own use with students.

GETTING STARTED

The first step is to register as an educator with SchoolTube by using the "For Educators" button at the top of the main page. When you log in for the first time, I suggest you browse through some videos to see how teachers are using this tool in their classrooms. The Videos page shows the most recently uploaded offerings, while the Channels page shows the channels that schools use for uploading. Finally, the Categories page divvies videos up into category topics for easy searching, such as "Elementary," "Music," "Health & Wellness," etc.

The next step is to produce your own video with a video camera. Any camera will do, as long as you are able to convert recordings into a movie file for upload. This site accepts the following video file types: 3GP, ASF, AVI, F4V, FLV, M4V, MOV, MP4, MPEG, MPG, RM, WMV, and Xvid. The vast majority of digital camera now record in one or more of these formats. Before pushing the "Record" button, however, it is important to develop a fun idea that students can utilize for learning. Students should develop the idea with a script and storyboard so they know exactly what they will be saying and doing before the camera starts rolling. Yes, you can edit out miscues later, but if the video primarily consists of miscues rather than real footage, editing becomes a very dragged out process. Start filming only when each and every student knows his or her role and expectations.

After gathering raw footage, the next step is to edit the video and produce a movie file for upload to SchoolTube. You can accomplish this in many different ways—if your school uses Windows PCs, Movie Maker is a good tool that comes packaged with Windows Me, XP, and Vista (Movie Maker's predecessor, Windows Live Movie Maker, is a free download for Windows 7). The same can be said for Macs and the application iMovie, which comes as part of the iLife suite with every Mac.

There are multitudes of other video production options that range in cost depending on the features and number of licenses you need. Look into these if you feel that Moviemaker or iMovie are not suiting your needs. Once you and your students have edited movies, they should be able to upload them to

SchoolTube (they will need an account as well to upload). Voila—a published video!

USE IN THE CLASSROOM

Producing and publishing digital video is an incredible way to empower your students as artists and thinkers. Students now are very familiar with video sharing sites because of YouTube, so SchoolTube is a natural fit for the classroom. Students can record and produce videos about any and all topics within your classroom, and you will be amazed at the creativity that will flow through their projects. They can conduct interviews, explore concepts, teach what they know to others who might be having trouble, and show what they know in a creative, meaningful way. Above all, make sure your students are able to express themselves creatively and have some fun with whatever project you're working on.

Students will thrive and excel when given the opportunity to showcase themselves and their talents to the world via SchoolTube. The publishing process itself leads to more motivated students in your classroom. Don't underestimate the difference you can make in your students' lives by publishing their videos, either.

OTHER ISSUES TO CONSIDER

→ TeacherTube is another resource to use with students. However, it is not moderated by educators and has struggled with speed issues in the past.

→ The first person at a school to sign up for SchoolTube becomes the default moderator. If your school will be using it a lot, this moderator may have a great deal of videos to sort through. You may want to divide these responsibilities among other teachers who sign up.

→ It is important to give students different tasks other than being in front of the camera—things like scripting, editing, research, etc. This helps incorporate all types of students into the process while addressing a greater array of multiple intelligences in the process.

→ If using SchoolTube to broadcast a regular news show, have students view the Broadcast Journalism Content Guidelines found on SchoolTube.

→ As moderator, you are responsible for making sure that every video uploaded at your school is appropriate. Make sure to read the SchoolTube Moderator guidelines before you moderate your first video.

→ Make sure to submit feedback if you have ideas to improve the site and vote on ideas that are already given so changes can be made quickly.

CONTENT AREA TIE-INS

Science

→ Give groups of students different physics concepts and ask them to create videos that illustrate each concept in some way (for example, demonstrate Isaac Newton's law of inertia with an air hockey table.)

→ Have students conduct an experiment and post it to SchoolTube.

Social Studies

→ Have students produce a video for the local school board, supporting the use of technology in schools.

→ Have students act out a famous battle that you are studying in class.

→ Host and record a town hall-style debate in your class on a current event.

SCREEN RECORDING

Language Arts

→ Record a video that leads students through learning how to write a style of poetry, such as haiku.

→ Have students record themselves as they edit a short paragraph. Encourage students to talk through the editing process and explain why they are changing or adding words, etc. When you review the video with them, discuss ways to improve their revision techniques.

→ Utilize the ability of students to teach and talk through the steps of any task they complete on the computer. Foreign language students can speak in the language they are studying, and ESL students can practice English in a real-world context.

Math

→ Have students open a drawing program and record themselves showing their work on an assigned problem. Show these videos to other students to illustrate multiple ways to solve the same problem.

→ Record and upload videos to your class website that show how to work through homework problems. Use any drawing program to do this—examples include MS Paint, Tux Paint (for younger students, available as a free download at **www. tuxpaint.org**), or Sumo Paint (free, Web-based drawing program located at **www. sumopaint.com**). Students can reference these at home if they get stuck.

→ Have a student that is an "expert" on a particular type of problem record an instructional video for the class.

GOAL: CREATE INSTRUCTIONAL VIDEOS BY SCREEN CAPTURING THE ACTIONS ON YOUR COMPUTER SCREEN.

OVERVIEW

Screen recording (also called screencasting) refers to the practice of using a piece of software to record a voice-narrated movie of whatever is happening on the computer screen at the time the record button is pressed. In fact, the videos on **www.edtechsteve.com** utilize screen-recording software. Utilizing screen-recording software can be an extremely helpful way to increase user understanding of computer-based tasks. In classrooms, it becomes a good way for students or teachers to explain concepts.

BUT FIRST...

→ Working with video requires a fast computer with decent graphics capabilities. A slow computer yields choppy video, and the processing time to produce the final product can be substantial.

→ Make sure you have a working microphone attached to your computer.

GETTING STARTED

There are many options for screen recording. Some are quite expensive. The software I used for the tutorial videos on my website is Camtasia Studio 6. At the time of this writing, the software retailed for $299, but was $179 for educators. If you plan on using advanced production methods, such as zooming in/out, adding transitions, effects, and the like, a paid version of screen recording software is preferable.

For regular classroom use with students, however, there are several high-quality, easy to use, free options as well. Some that I've tried successfully are CamStudio (**www.camstudio.org**), Jing (**www.jingproject.com**), and Screenr (**www.screenr.com**). All of these products offer the same, simple functionality. Some differences are outlined in the "Other Issues to Consider" section. To best decide which you prefer, you might want to download each and give them a try.

Once you've installed a program, the next step in the process is recording a rectangular section or all of your screen. After you click on the record button and specify your choice to record, recording will begin. At that moment, whatever you do with your mouse will be recorded and, if you have a microphone, your voice will be as well. In this way, you can click and narrate whatever is pulled up on your screen. When you are finished, hit the "Stop" button. A dialog box will come up, asking you what you want to name your movie and where you'd like to save it.

USE IN THE CLASSROOM

Screen recording can be a powerful classroom tool for both teacher- and student-created projects. On the teacher side, screen recording provides extra support for your students. For teaching particularly difficult or complex concepts, create a screen recording that talks the students through the process. This video can then be posted online so your students can refer to it when they need help.

For students, what better way is there to learn a concept than by teaching it themselves? Screen recording software allows them to do just that. They record their own video that teaches a process or outlines information presented on their screen. This video can then be shown or provided to other students in the class. Often, our students can explain activities better than we can… why not let them?

OTHER ISSUES TO CONSIDER

→ In Jing, PC users will need to install Microsoft .NET Framework 3.5 SP1 software to run the program. This is a 2.8 MB download; the entire Jing program is 6.60 MB. Mac users have a different list of requirements, viewable here: **http://www.techsmith.com/download/jing**.

→ The free version of Jing only allows you to save the video files in an Adobe Flash format (SWF). CamStudio allows you to save as an AVI file. AVI files are more widely compatible and easier to edit (they can be edited in Windows Movie Maker, for example).

→ Screenr posts directly to your Twitter account, so you can very easily share your screencasts with the world.

→ Once you have recorded your screencast, the movie file can be edited; you can pull clips from it, add transitions, and publish as other types of files. Video editing software such as Microsoft Movie Maker or iMovie are needed to utilize this function.

→ Screen recording is a perfect match with software that comes with interactive whiteboards, such as SMART Notebook (comes with SMART Board) or ActivInspire (comes with Promethean boards). Turn the recording on, and utilize the tools within these programs to outline concepts.

→ Save good videos to use with future classes. There is certainly no need to reinvent the wheel every year, so hang onto the good ones for future use!

I love using screencasting tools with my students to publish my students' work on their blogs and on our class wiki... Screencasting is simple to do, but powerful because the tools create an embed code; students can easily share their projects with the world.

MICHAEL KAECHELE
Technology & Math

CONTENT AREA TIE-INS

Science

→ Record a video that leads students through navigation of a science museum website such as the Exploratorium (**www.exploratorium.edu**) or the Smithsonian Institute (**www.si.edu**).

→ Have students record a video of themselves as they perform an online dissection (See a model of this at Froguts: **www.dissect.froguts.com**).

Social Studies

→ Record a video that shows students how to navigate the Library of Congress website (**www.loc.gov**) or other sites that offer rich information related to the topic at hand.

→ Have students talk through the events of a timeline they create on their computer (see the timeline tool activity on p. 82).

TOOL #19
SECOND LIFE

CONTENT AREA TIE-INS

Language Arts

→ Create and build a non-fiction character with the appearance editor within Second Life. Students choose an aspect of the avatar's appearance to change and, as a class, talk about how this change might affect this character in a story (For example, if the students choose to give the character long facial hair, what might that mean for him if they were to use him in a story?)

→ Attend author readings within Second Life. Many authors have presences in Second Life, which offers opportunities to interact with them on a whole new level. For example, bestselling writer Dean Koontz appeared in Second Life and read an excerpt from an upcoming book.

Math

→ Use Second Life to illustrate exchange rates. Users can exchange real dollars for virtual world Linden Dollars from the Second Life site. Exchange rates change online just as they do in real banks, so students can determine the exchange rate and work on problems based on currency ("If you have $325, how many Lindens could you purchase?")

→ View and discuss Second Life's statistics for the following: amount of land sold, Linden Dollars spent, number of users, monthly customer spending, and other data points. These raw numbers can be found in Excel spreadsheets available for download on the website (**www.secondlife.com/statistics/economy-data.php**).

OVERVIEW

Second Life is a free, downloadable program that allows users to create an avatar (a virtual self) and enter an interactive virtual world. As an avatar, you are able to connect with other avatars created by people around the world. Within this virtual environment, you can explore buildings, obtain information about a wide variety of topics, create objects, buy land, and even buy and sell virtual goods! Second Life is built by users from all over the planet who log in and create virtual spaces for many different purposes: online universities, conference hosting, dance parties, band demos, and almost anything else you can imagine.

Within Second Life, there is an entire economy based on virtual money. The currency in Second Life is called Linden Dollars (named after the company that created the program, Linden Labs). Users can exchange real money for Linden Dollars, which are then used by your avatar to purchase virtual items within the Second Life world. It might be hard to imagine that people exchange real money with virtual money to purchase virtual items, but it is extremely popular!

BUT FIRST...

→ This tool is graphics-intensive, and it needs a pretty powerful computer to run fluidly. Second Life will automatically detect and adjust your settings for maximum usability.

→ A quick warning: Second Life offers all sorts of educational opportunities, but it also mirrors the Internet in general; there are many inappropriate places and people, so be wary.

GETTING STARTED

You will need to install Second Life on your computer, so the first step is to head to **www.secondlife.com** and download the program. To do this, click the "Join Now" button on the homepage. Register by entering your basic information, choosing a name, and creating your avatar. Keep in mind that your name is permanent once chosen, but not your appearance. After confirming your e-mail address, Second Life prompts you to download and install the program.

After installation, start it up and log in. Once logged in, the program takes you to a very useful place: Help Island. As you might imagine, Help Island leads you through all of the basics you need to know. Make sure to learn how to fly, move, change your appearance, use your inventory, and interact with others via text and voice chat. Have fun playing around with your avatar and making him or her look the way you want.

Once you have learned the basics on Help Island, you can enter the realm, otherwise known as the Second Life main grid, by teleportation. On the main grid, begin exploring. You can simply hit the "Map" button and start teleporting to different spots. Within the map, landmarks are visible and other users are illustrated by green circles. To teleport to a new spot, simply double-click one.

Second Life also features many interesting locations on the bottom of their homepage. Simply scroll down and select "Destination Guide." All locations within the program are represented by what are called "SLurls." When clicked, these links will teleport you directly to that spot within the program.

USE IN THE CLASSROOM

In lean economic times and tight budgets, more and more universities and conferences are looking toward moving to a purely online format for courses and presentations. Second Life provides an interactive environment that is highly customizable to the needs of users. For this reason, it should only continue to grow as an educational tool, not only for students but also for teachers and administrators who want to expand their personal learning networks.

A growing familiarity with online, virtual worlds is another reason Second Life is growing as a tool to use in the classroom. Kids already are well acquainted with virtual environments like Webkinz, The Sims, or World of Warcraft. It only makes sense to apply that interest and comfort to the learning environment.

The collaborative aspect of Second Life is unparalleled. Students can listen to presentations or converse with people anywhere in the world, which provides a powerful, real-life illustration of the "flattening" of today's world. Many teachers also report that forging new relationships is the main benefit of using Second Life. The conversations to be had within Second Life can lead to personal and professional development.

And, finally, Second Life offers some amazing opportunities for your students to explore places they might not ever physically visit. Through Second Life, they can virtually visit art museums, experience virtual hurricane demonstrations, view the work of Frank Lloyd Wright, and much, much more. The following ideas only scratch the surface as to what is available to explore in Second Life!

OTHER ISSUES TO CONSIDER

→ You will be surprised at how many organizations and companies have spaces within Second Life. Just search within Second Life for their presence.

→ The main grid of Second Life is restricted to eighteen-plus. This means that any interaction with Second Life for students in your classroom will have to be a whole-group activity, driven and guided by you. Students should never have the opportunity to create a login or explore the main grid at school.

→ To purchase clothing, accessories, and even land using Linden Dollars, visit **www.xstreetsl.com**.

→ Others can crash the party while you are exploring as a class! You can stop others from communicating with you, however, by turning text and voice chat communications off under Edit/Preferences. This is highly recommended when leading a class through a public site.

→ Teen Grid or Teen Second Life is available for those aged thirteen to seventeen. It is restricted to these ages only. Many educational initiatives are now being formed on the Teen Grid, as it is shielded from much of the inappropriate material found within the main grid of Second Life.

CONTENT AREA TIE-INS

Science

→ Have students download data and analyze trends, create graphs, etc. Visit the National Oceanic and Atmospheric Administration's Second Life presence at the following SLurl: **www.slurl.com/ secondlife/Meteora/177/161/27**. Here, students can see real-time weather maps, take a "hurricane ride," look at types of sea life, and interact with a weather balloon and glacier to learn more about both.

→ Visit the International Spaceflight Museum, a museum existing only in Second Life that hosts events about real-world spacecraft and space travel at: **www. slurl.com/secondlife/Spaceport%20 Alpha/48/78/24**.

Social Studies

→ Visit the Latino Virtual Smithsonian Museum, a Second Life project of the Smithsonian Latino Center (find out more at **www.latino.si.edu/education/ LVM_Main.htm**). Here, students can view photos, see virtual recreations of buildings, and find other information about Latino art, music, dancing, and other cultural aspects.

→ Explore the many countries that now have embassy spaces within Second Life for people to visit and gain information. Just do an Internet search for a country's name and "Second Life" to see if they are represented. Several states do as well!

→ Study different landforms such as mountains, rivers, lakes, islands, and valleys by "teleporting" to different locations.

TOOL #20

SLIDESHARE

OVERVIEW

SlideShare (**www.slideshare.net**) is an online tool that allows users to publish a wide variety of PDF, presentation, word processing, or spreadsheet documents. Once published, other users can comment on the presentations. These published documents can also be selected and embedded into social networking sites such as Facebook, Blogger, WordPress, Twitter, or Delicious. What this effectively does is add a social networking aspect to informational presentations, and it allows them to be shared, rated, commented on, and downloaded by others. Another important component of SlideShare is that it's searchable. Need a presentation on the Civil War? There are hundreds!

BUT FIRST...

→ To play slideshows within the site, download the latest version of Adobe Flash (**www.adobe.com/products/flashplayer**).

GETTING STARTED

Once you register, the process begins quite easily: just click on the "Upload" button and you are given the choice to upload your files. After the files are uploaded, you will be prompted to enter file details, such as the title, description, what category it belongs in, who can view it, and what tags it should be associated with. Once you enter the information, hit the "Publish" button. The file will then be converted by SlideShare and uploaded to the site.

Once on SlideShare, there are many things you can do with your file. You can embed it into Blogger, Facebook, WordPress, Twitter, or Delicious by simply clicking on the corresponding button next to the show and entering your information for each. You can share this presentation with students or colleagues by adding their e-mails and a custom message. You can add an MP3 you have recorded of yourself to play throughout the presentation to narrate the slidecast. You can even insert YouTube videos into your presentation. All of these tools enhance the presentation and help make it a more interactive experience.

USE IN THE CLASSROOM

SlideShare has many uses in the classroom. The first and most obvious is the ability to publish presentations to the Web that your students have already created via PowerPoint. Once published (either through student accounts or uploaded by you, the teacher), students can access each other's presentations anywhere they have an Internet connection. From here, they can comment on other presentations that have been uploaded.

SlideShare is also a great research tool. There are thousands of presentations on a wide variety of subjects already created and ready to be viewed. This can be an excellent way for students to find well-done, succinct presentations on any topic they are currently studying. They can even download multiple presentation files about the same topic and merge parts to create something that suits their needs.

If you are feeling adventurous, get your students to slidecast. As defined by SlideShare, slidecasting combines SlideShare slides with MP3 podcasting.

CONTENT AREA TIE-INS

Language Arts

→ Have students create a slidecast of one of their own, original stories. They create the slides with the text and/or pictures and record their own voice to tell the story.

→ Ask students to create and publish presentations about the genre of their favorite books using example passages from each type of book.

→ Let students create a poem and set it up as a slideshow, then share it with the world and solicit comments.

Math

→ Let students create and publish presentations that instruct their parents/guardians how to do the math concepts they are currently being taught.

→ Group students according to the way they approach a certain type of problem. The groups create and publish presentations detailing their particular solution. Students from other groups view alternative solutions and comment on whether or not this approach to solving the problem works for them.

→ Have students create and publish presentations that cover math concepts they have been working on, such as different types of triangles, finding areas of different shapes, etc.

Basically, you are able to upload a podcast that narrates the slide presentation, then synchronize the audio and slideshow. This is another engaging way to have your students show what they know!

OTHER ISSUES TO CONSIDER

→ Presentation animations do not translate to SlideShare. In other words, no flying in, wiping across, or faded zooms.

→ Some educators are still hesitant to allow students to pull information from other people's slides and adapt them. I encourage you to allow your students to pull slides, rearrange and edit them, add their own flair, etc. This "mashup" is a primary way for this generation of students to express themselves. Discussing the choices they made as to what to pick and pull can offer excellent insight into their thinking processes.

→ Allow students to be creative with their presentations! This is a good opportunity to allow for lots of customization. Try not to focus on limiting the aesthetics of the presentation as long as they satisfy content expectations.

→ As with all products, if your students use someone else's presentation in any way they should cite the creator.

CONTENT AREA TIE-INS

Science

→ Create a slidecast about how tornadoes or hurricanes form and the damage they can cause.

→ Have students create presentations that detail the layers of the earth.

→ Ask students to create and publish presentations that show the effects of smoking or drug use on the human body.

Social Studies

→ Ask students to create and publish presentations that deal with making an impact in some way, such a persuading people in their community to be more energy-efficient, for example.

→ Have small groups take different positions on a current event. Each group creates and publishes a persuasive presentation that outlines their beliefs.

→ Search SlideShare to find presentations published by students who live in the foreign countries you are studying.

TOOL #21

SPORE CREATURE CREATOR

CONTENT AREA TIE-INS

Language Arts

→ Have students build fantasy creatures that they incorporate into creative writing pieces. As students add parts, have them jot down how those parts could affect the way their creature behaves in their story (for example, if the creature only has one eye, perhaps it's clumsy; or, maybe it looks like a savage killer but is really a big teddy bear.) Insert pictures of the creature into the story to remind both the author and the reader what the character looks like.

→ Let students recreate an animal or fantasy creature from a novel the class is studying or from a book they enjoy.

→ Have students write descriptive paragraphs based on the creature and its distinguishing features (this works well with language learners as well—ESL students can learn the English words for parts of the body).

→ Have students work in pairs where each one brings in a picture of the creature he or she created. Ask students to compare/contrast the creatures and write a short story together about their creatures meeting.

Social Studies

→ Find an animal that plays a crucial part in the local economic, political, or social dynamics of an area of the world you are studying, and attempt to recreate it. This can be done either with individual students, pairs, small groups, or as a class activity.

→ Have students make a creature they believe would thrive in a particular country and its associated landforms. Make sure students can justify the choices they've made and reconcile them with what they've learned about that area of the world.

GOAL: STUDENTS CREATE INTERESTING CREATURES THAT ACTIVATE THEIR THINKING PROCESSES.

OVERVIEW

The Spore Creature Creator is a free piece of the larger retail game, Spore. Within the program, students are able to create just about any type of creature they can envision by adding various appendages, sensory organs, weapons, and other various body parts. These parts and the body itself are all entirely customizable. They can be moved, distorted, bent, and even made larger or smaller.

After the creature is created, it can be colored/detailed and taken for a "test drive" to see how it would move and interact with others. Finally, pictures and video can be taken of the creature to extend its life into other learning applications.

BUT FIRST...

→ This is a free program, but even so it may take some convincing to get your IT department to put it onto either stand-alone or lab computers. You may need to set up an appointment with whoever makes these decisions so you can show them the benefits of the program and how you plan to use it with your students.

→ In Windows PCs, this program requires the latest version of the program, DirectX. When installing, it will prompt you to install DirectX if you do not already have it. Mac systems do not require this.

GETTING STARTED

The free version of the Creature Creator is available for both Windows PC and Mac and can be downloaded from **www.spore.com**. Just click the "Try Now" button to begin. Download and install the program on whatever computer(s) you plan to use.

When you start the program, it will prompt you to register. Note that registration is not required for students to use Creature Creator, so you can simply cancel out of this prompt. Click on "Build a Creature" and you are ready to begin.

The controls for the Creature Creator are easy to understand. When you hover over the torso, you will see vertebrae. Simply click and drag the vertebrae to shape the torso however you'd like. Click and drag the red arrows to lengthen and shorten your creature. You can also make any part of the body larger or smaller by rolling the mouse wheel back and forth over it. You can do this with every part, including vertebrae!

Next, add body parts. Along the left-hand side of the screen, you will see several categories of parts (mouths, arms, legs, graspers, etc.) Choose a part, then drag it to where you want it to attach to the torso. Once the part is placed, you will see arrows, circles, and sometimes rings around the parts. These figures point out even more ways to customize the creature. Take a little time to play with these features, and you will quickly see how easily changes can be made.

After you have your parts finished, it is time to paint the creature by clicking on the paintbrush at the top of the screen. When finished, click on the button with the tracks on it to take your creature for a "test drive" and see how it moves, points, interacts with others, and even how it dances!

Lastly, when in test drive mode, you will see some excellent functions–the camera and the camcorder buttons. The camera button takes a picture of your creature and places it into a folder in My Documents, titled "My Spore Creations." If you click the camcorder button, a video is recorded and saved in the same place. These pictures and videos can then be imported and used in other programs (PowerPoint, Photo Story, Movie Maker, MS Word, Excel, Publisher, etc.)

USE IN THE CLASSROOM
Because Spore fully engages students with the topic at hand while allowing them to have fun and be creative, it's an excellent learning tool. It essentially puts animation tools in their hands that had previously only been available to game designers. The variety of creatures your students will come up with will astonish you; who knows, you may create the next group of video game artists.

The most exciting aspect of using Spore in the classroom is that it allows students to create customized creatures that can be use as a springboard to increase their understanding of many concepts you are trying to get across. Students can make these creatures individually or as a whole group using one computer and projector. The flexibility within the program allows you to utilize it in many different ways.

OTHER ISSUES TO CONSIDER
→   The free version of the Creature Creator program differs from the full version only in the number of body parts that can be applied. In the free version, you will see one row of parts with the other rows replaced by question marks. If you purchase the full version (just $10), all of the other parts will be unlocked. You can also purchase an add-on from Spore called "Creepy & Cute" that adds an additional sixty parts, forty eight color styles, and twenty four new "test drive" animations, including the moonwalk.

→   The full version of the game, Spore, is an excellent tool as well. Within the game, you build your creature through five stages of life: cell, creature, tribe, civilization, and space. Each stage offers unique learning opportunities, as well as the opportunity to create not just creatures, but cars, airplanes, buildings, boats, tribal outfits, and more!

CONTENT AREA TIE-INS

Science
→   Use these creatures for any animal adaptations study. They offer the opportunity for rich discussion about types of teeth, camouflage, weaponry, decorative parts to attract mates, grasping fingers, webbed feet, etc.

→   Use creatures to teach about genetics. Assign characteristics, such as type of claw or number of horns as dominant or recessive traits and have students build a genome that they can then attempt to create within the Creature Creator.

→   Create creatures to discuss varying climates and habitats. What characteristics would be common to a creature living in the desert? The rain forest? The Rocky Mountains?

Math
→   Graph and compare student creations. When creating creatures, the parts you add have traits and ratings (a mouth may have a Level 3 sing and a Level 4 bite). These traits can be used as percentages ("What percent of our class created a creature with a Level 3+ Singing Ability?") or ratios.

→   Have students create word problems associated with their creatures. Problems could include number of legs, eyes, arms, fingers, etc.

→   Print cards out of the creatures by inserting their pictures into MS Word or other word processing software. Use these cards for graphing, sorting, or Venn diagrams.

TIMELINE CREATORS

CONTENT AREA TIE-INS

Language Arts

→ Ask students to create a timeline that represents a book they are reading. If the book does not contain specific years, teach students how to infer time from descriptive settings (and how they can use this technique in their own writing).

→ Utilize a timeline as part of an author study.

→ Have each student pick a subject about which to create a timeline—any subject at all. The catch is that they must use highly descriptive language when adding events.

Math

→ Share a topic-of-study timeline for the year with your students and their parents. This can be shown as a link on your class website or embedded right into it.

→ Ask students to browse and find interesting timelines. When they've found one, ask them to analyze it mathematically; for example, what are the average number of days between each event, what is the range, what percent or fraction of events includes a picture? You could also pose time-related word problems such as, "If you were thirty four years old when the second timeline event occurred, how old would you be by the last event?"

GOAL: STUDENTS CREATE INTERACTIVE TIMELINES FOR PUBLICATION.

OVERVIEW

Timeline creators allow you and your students to create interactive timelines that are housed online. The timelines include specific dates and pictures, as well as added information that expands for each event. Each timeline creation tool is easy to use and allows you to show and sequence events related to your content area.

BUT FIRST...

→ These tools require the latest version of Adobe Flash on each computer.

GETTING STARTED

There are many choices for timeline creators, and they all work in much the same way. Students can add event titles, dates, descriptions, and images or other media to coincide with each event. I've selected some of the best current choices. Try a few to see which fits your style or students' needs the most:

1. Timetoast (most visually pleasing): **www.timetoast.com**
2. TimeRime (easy and visually pleasing): **www.timerime.com**
3. Xtimeline (easiest to set up): **www.xtimeline.com**
4. Preceden (allows overlapping events): **www.preceden.com**

After registering, your students can simply start adding events. The events should include a title, description, date, and (with all tools except Preceden) an optional image. The timeline is created after all the event information has been entered. Students can easily do all this individually, in pairs, or in small groups—whatever fits your classroom needs best.

Once a timeline has been created, your students' work can be shared or embedded onto other sites by using the code provided. In addition, your students can share their timelines as a link, via e-mail, or through social networking sites such as Facebook, MySpace, and Twitter.

USE IN THE CLASSROOM

Timelines are useful in every subject. Putting events in chronological order helps with sequencing skills by allowing us to view a progression of events and put them into perspective. Good descriptive language skills are also inherently important to create a useful timeline; students need to describe clearly and concisely what happened at a single point in time. Timelines can be used to describe a wide range of subjects and should not just be delegated to history and biography. The public timelines housed on each of these sites are also searchable, which means you can use these sites as great resources for students to conduct research on class topics. Simply look for categories of timelines on each site and browse/search from there.

OTHER ISSUES TO CONSIDER

→ The maximum size for images in Timetoast is 3 MB. If you are selecting digital pictures from your computer, some of them may need to be resized beforehand.

→ One big advantage of using Preceden is that it allows users to create layers within the timeline. Students can then see how events overlap or coincide.

→ As of this writing, Timetoast only allows A.D. events. The site states that a B.C. feature will soon be added.

→ TimeRime offers educator accounts, for a fee. These accounts allow teachers more power and control over the management of their students' timelines.

Before they had access to the Web, students would purchase poster board, brightly colored paper, and markers to create timelines. Timelines created in Timetoast not only look good, but they also have features that make them useful for learning. For example, students can enter images and text about an event on the timeline and add links to more information about the event or cite resources.

STEVEN ANDERSON
Instructional Technologist

CONTENT AREA TIE-INS

Science

→ Create a timeline that shows the discovery of a new animal species in the past twenty years, with descriptions that include images of the animal, who discovered it, where it was found, etc.

→ Ask students to create a timeline of the deadliest instances of different types of extreme weather (all Category Five hurricanes in the past fifty years, for example).

→ Take a scientific slant on a current event and ask students to create a timeline describing it. Examples could be the development of solar energy, the history of stem cell research, etc.

Social Studies

→ Have each student choose a significant monument or building and research/create a timeline about its construction and other significant happenings relating to the monument.

→ Ask students to create timelines that track an invention that had a large impact on society.

→ Create timelines that show the root issues involved with current news items (for example, how did the economic crisis in 2008 start?)

→ Have students conduct time-related research by searching for timelines with each timeline creator's browse feature.

TODAYSMEET

Language Arts

→ Create rooms based on one aspect of language, for example literary devices. Students log in at home or at school and contribute phrases from their reading that illustrate the device.

→ Use TodaysMeet for collaborative story writing. Project the chat room to the front of the room to get started. Next, assign numbers to each student and have them create sentences in sequence, building upon each other's thoughts. Note how the story developed, discuss whether or not this is effective, and point out good uses of language within the sentences that are offered.

→ Create chat rooms that are used for book chats about the novels you are reading in class.

→ Conduct a "Vocabulary Race." You supply a word, and students race to find and post the definition in the chat room. Students could also post the part of speech, word origin, or spelling of the word.

Math

→ Keep a chat room open as a backchannel for students to post questions about the material being presented.

→ Use TodaysMeet to conduct online office hours for homework help. Half an hour or more during a week would be of great help to students (and parents who struggle with helping their student in math).

→ Use the room to promote quick thinking. Students race to solve a math problem and be the first to post the answer in the chat room. Check to see who got it right. If you discover several similar, incorrect answers, you can discuss and help students correct the commonly made mistakes.

GOAL: STUDENTS CREATE AND USE AN EASY, ACCESSIBLE CHAT ENVIRONMENT.

OVERVIEW

TodaysMeet (**www.todaysmeet.com**) is a fantastic new tool that easily creates a functional chat environment. It takes advantage of a growing movement in classrooms, conferences, and professional development sessions: the creation of a "backchannel."

A backchannel is simply a place where participants chat with each other about what is being presented. Think of it as the new "back of the room" conversation. For so long, the idea of these "sidebar" conversations have been looked down upon because it seems as though the participants/students aren't listening. In reality, however, most of these conversations do revolve around the topic or idea being presented.

Taking advantage of this and providing an environment in which those conversations can occur in a constructive way can be a powerful tool. Imagine being able to read the real-time thoughts of your students! With TodaysMeet, you can do just that.

GETTING STARTED

As of this writing, no registration is required, which makes TodaysMeet easy to pick up and use right away. Once at the site, simply give the room a name, tell the site how long you want the room to exist, and click "Create your Room." This takes you directly to the message section. After each participating user logs on and enters his or her name, it is time to start chatting. One thing to keep in mind is that entering text is similar to Twitter; you are only allowed 140 characters per comment (note the ticker above the textbox that counts down as you type).

Besides being simple to use, the way TodaysMeet easily creates a unique URL is very helpful. Typically, it simply adds the room's name to the end of the root site's name (todaysmeet.com/booktest, for example). This allows the link to be shared easily within large or small groups.

Finally, TodaysMeet can also be used through Twitter hashtags (for more information on Twitter and hashtags, go to the outline of Twitter found on p. 86). By incorporating these hashtags, participants can follow a group Twitter conversation through TodaysMeet.

USE IN THE CLASSROOM

An easy-to-use chat room environment is a powerful classroom learning tool. In the chat room, students can openly discuss ideas, thoughts, and concepts you are working on in class. If used as a backchannel, it gives you real-time insights about students' thoughts and feelings about the material you're presenting, enabling you to adjust your teaching accordingly. You can also utilize TodaysMeet as an ongoing persistent discussion space inside and outside of class for up to one year. Students are going to have these thoughts and conversations anyway, so why not utilize them to create a better and more responsive learning environment?

Keep in mind that in order to use this tool, students are going to have to connect to the internet in some way. This can be through the use of computers (in a computer lab), laptops (if you have some in your room), or even mobile devices such as an iPod Touch or cell phone.

OTHER ISSUES TO CONSIDER

→ Messages are not instantaneous. It can sometimes take a few seconds for a posted comment to register in the chat room.

→ Students can put *anything* into the name area, and the site will not filter inappropriate words. It is up to you as the teacher to set guidelines and limits, as well as monitor use closely.

→ A transcript is provided by clicking the "transcript" link at the bottom of the chat space. This allows you to track conversations that occur outside of the classroom.

→ Another chat room creator that works well is Chatzy, located at **www.chatzy.com**. This option is not as straightforward and easy as TodaysMeet, but it does offer a few more options to customize the room itself. There is also no transcript option available in Chatzy as of the writing of this book.

CONTENT AREA TIE-INS

Science

→ Utilize the chat room's ability to elicit quick responses about possible hypotheses when conducting experiments. You can do the same with observations, either as a class or in lab small groups.

→ Post a diagram of a cell (or anything else that students might need to know the parts of) at the front of the room, and challenge your class to post every part they know. Do this at the beginning and end of a study to see how much they've improved (and have fun with the names they give the parts they haven't learned about yet!)

→ Keep a backchannel chat room open when viewing movies as a class. Allow students to post questions or comments within the room, and stop frequently if questions need answering.

Social Studies

→ Have students recreate famous debates within TodaysMeet. For example, students could log into TodaysMeet as various members of the Constitutional Convention and debate ideas as if they were members of Congress back in 1787.

→ Hold debates about current issues within TodaysMeet by picking a relevant topic and collecting opinions in this format. Push students to summarize the points and counterpoints when the chat is completed.

→ Show a video clip of any topic you are studying, and open TodaysMeet as a backchannel to discuss what they are seeing. Allow students to chat with each other about the contents of the video, and use the comments to draw conclusions when the video ends.

TOOL #24

TWITTER

Language Arts

→ Give "word of the day" updates: new vocabulary words for the upcoming week. Give bonus points in class to students that can use them appropriately in everyday classroom discussion.

→ Look up and "follow" famous authors or writers who the class is currently studying.

→ Compare and contrast traditional messages versus tweets.

→ Examine word usage on Twitter via TweetVolume (**www.tweetvolume.com**). This allows you to see what types of words are being used most frequently on Twitter over the past day, week, and year. Encourage discussion on trending words or phrases.

Math

→ Pose word problems over Twitter for students to solve and reply to.

→ Pull math concepts from mashups that analyze Twitter accounts. Try these sites to gather usage statistics: Twitterholic (**www.twitterholic.com**), TweetStats (**www.tweetstats.com**), and TwitterCounter (**www.twittercounter.com**). Utilize these stats in a variety of ways—for example, as comparisons, rations, percentages, graphs, etc.

→ Ask students to post brainteasers on their Twitter accounts and report back if any of their followers were able to solve them.

GOAL: TO ESTABLISH CONNECTIONS AND COMMUNICATION TO A WIDE AUDIENCE.

OVERVIEW

What started out as a relatively small blip on the social networking radar has evolved into a powerful tool used for much more than the simple, "What's happening?" prompt it is now famous for. Twitter is what is known as micro-blogging: paring down thoughts, ideas, actions, etc., into messages that are restricted to 140 characters or less.

Twitter started as a relatively harmless way to give you the ability to tell friends that follow your updates what you are doing throughout the day. As more and more users flooded to the site, however, it morphed into a powerful (some would argue world-changing) force. Most famously, the Twitter users ("tweeps") became on-the-spot journalists who have covered major events, such as the disputed Iranian presidential elections of June 2009. News of these events flowed through Twitter and other social networking sites, and Iranians were able to get firsthand accounts out to the world as they happened, often with vivid pictures and video–despite the official Iranian government lock-down of all media coverage of the event.

The ability to access Twitter from mobile devices has led to an explosion of new uses. Primary among these for teachers is the ability to share resources and ideas among a network of friends (your PLN). Twitter has also emerged as a marketing tool for companies all across the globe, large and small, changing how companies do business and interact with their customers. Users are able to tag words in their posts, making them searchable. Twitter means instant communication and a way to bridge distance and social gaps.

GETTING STARTED

Head to **www.twitter.com** and create an account. Whatever username you choose will be your new Twitter address (for example, my username is edtechsteve so my URL address for Twitter is **www.twitter.com/edtechsteve**). Once you are logged in, it's time to send your first tweet (message). Simply click in the empty box under the question, "What's happening?" As you type, you will notice the 140 character ticker running out for each letter or space you enter. Once you're done typing (and as long as it is under the 140 character limit), just hit "Tweet."

This is just the beginning, however. After all, what use would it be to sit around and type to yourself all day? The next thing you should do is find some people to "follow". These could be friends, family, colleagues, institutions, the President, celebrities, or any number of people you choose. You can find people to follow in several ways. A "Find People" feature inside Twitter allows a search for names or usernames. Another great tactic is to go to a person's page you really respect and see who they are following. Finally, a good rule of thumb is to check out a person's page before you start to follow them to see if they interest you, what types of things they post, and if they post too often or not enough for your taste. If you decide you'd like to follow what they have to offer, simply click the "Follow" button on their page.

Twitter also gives you the ability to follow groups of people, ideas, or conduct live chats with many users from around the world, accomplished through what is known as "hashtagging." To apply a hashtag to a Twitter post, all you have to do is add the hashtag symbol: #. For example, let's say that every Tuesday night from 7:00-8:00 p.m. EST, there is an #edchat discussion.

Users who wish to participate in this discussion add the #edchat hashtag to their posts within Twitter. Then, whoever would like to follow or participate in the conversation can search Twitter for "#edchat," which will list all the posts that contain that tag. In this way, you can follow a large number of people who are discussing the same topic.

You can also reply to someone's tweet or privately direct-message him or her; you can even "retweet" a post that you find interesting and believe whoever is following you would also like to see. All of this can be done via the Twitter website or through free Twitter client programs (such as TweetDeck or twhirl), or from a cell phone. As you can see, the opportunities for instant communication wherever, whenever are nearly endless.

USE IN THE CLASSROOM

Because Twitter has become a part of our culture, it should not be ignored in schools. A school Twitter account provides a great way to keep parents, students, and the community at large informed about school events and courses. Teachers can also create an account to give information about upcoming tests and use the account as yet another way to praise students in a public forum. A simple "Great job today with rain forest presentations!" will be appreciated by your students and their families.

Twitter can also be used to help students write with clarity and brevity. As you use Twitter more and more, you'll naturally start to develop a highly metacognitive thinking process about your posts. You start to think to yourself, "How can I convey this thought or feeling succinctly and clearly in 140 characters or less?" This is a great skill for students to obtain and maintain.

And finally, as mentioned earlier in this book, Twitter is an excellent addition to one's Personal Learning Network. Take advantage of the enormous community of educator colleagues who are responsive and willing to support your professional growth.

OTHER ISSUES TO CONSIDER

→ When creating a Twitter account, it's a good idea to separate the personal from professional by creating two accounts for yourself. On your school account, remember to always remain professional in your interactions with students and colleagues. Everything you write on Twitter can be accessed from someone, somewhere. Remember, there is no "taking it back" once it is out there.

→ People and companies generally use Twitter for self-serving reasons. If you're "following" an author, for example, be prepared to read about his or her current projects, conferences, etc.

→ Don't be intimidated by the lingo surrounding Twitter! It may seem like another language, but remember the concept is truly simple: people posting their ideas, thoughts, and resources.

→ Many useful tools have emerged to manage the sometimes overwhelming Twitter update feed. Two useful ways of tracking hashtag discussions are TweetChat (**www.tweetchat.com**) and TweetGrid (**www.tweetgrid.com**).

CONTENT AREA TIE-INS

Science

→ Follow National Geographic on Twitter at **www.twitter.com/NatGeoSociety** for links to amazing photos, videos, and articles.

→ Have students micro-blog about their thoughts and observations while conducting field experiments.

Social Studies

→ Let students imagine and write as a historical figure. What would he or she tweet about? Place figures in the context of your study, and see what students come up with (for example, Abraham Lincoln in July 1862).

→ Have an imaginary tweet debate between two opposing sides set in context. For example, W.E.B. Du Bois versus Booker T. Washington.

→ Have students follow current events within Twitter by searching topics on **www. search.twitter.com**.

→ Discuss the impact of Twitter and other instant communication on current events and what this means for the future of economics, politics, global awareness, etc.

VIDEO CONFERENCING

CONTENT AREA TIE-INS

Language Arts

→ Video conference with an author. Many authors are now available to video conference with your students (for relatively cheap, as well). You can either contact the author individually through his or her publisher, or use the Skype an Author Network as a starting point: **www.skypeanauthor. wetpaint.com**. I would enjoy speaking to your class on a variety of topics as well. You can find my Skype contact information on **www.edtechsteve.com**.

→ Build a collaborative story with students from another class. Think of this as a "whisper down the lane" activity, where one side starts a story then switches to the other side for the next piece. This back-and-forth narrative can provide a fascinating look at how different cultures rely on different themes in storytelling.

→ Take advantage of the many vocabulary- and language acquisition-building opportunities within a Web conference. Students can provide challenge words to each other, or play language games like hangman, word scramble, etc.

Social Studies

→ Connect with other cultures that you are studying. Ask students to give summaries of what they expect from students in that country. Then, after connecting, talk about whether or not those expectations were right or wrong.

→ Have students prepare questions for the other class regarding the structure of their government, local politics, etc. Ask your students to prepare the same information to show visually.

→ Have students from two classes show each other a favorite game or pastime.

GOAL: TO CONNECT WITH OTHERS VIA LIVE VIDEO STREAMED OVER THE INTERNET.

OVERVIEW

Video conferencing refers to two parties with Web cameras connecting over the Internet to share both video and voice. Over the last decade, it's come a long way–from scratchy and expensive to clear and cheap! Most laptops now come with a built-in webcam, and even computers without this feature can add a high-quality camera for under $50. Even better, the software to run webconferences is now 100 percent free worldwide. This gives you and your students the chance to easily interact with others through voice chat, whether they're down the street or on the other side of the world.

BUT FIRST...

→ You will need a webcam and a computer/laptop with a built-in webcam.

GETTING STARTED

Webcam in hand, you need to choose the software you will use to connect with others via the Internet. Although there are many free options, as of this writing Skype (**www.skype.com**) stands above the rest as far as video quality, features, and ease of use. After registering and installing the program, you can add your contact information as well as send e-mails to friends, encouraging them install the program themselves.

After they register, your contacts will show up in your Skype window. From there, simply click on the name of the person you'd like to video conference with and hit the "Call" button (in Skype, this button is a green phone). For a list of other programs that work in a similar manner, look at the first bullet below under "Other Issues to Consider."

USE IN THE CLASSROOM

Preparation is key to classroom success with video conferencing. You can't simply turn the webcam on and expect your students to ask relevant questions or probe a topic. They should know what they want to get out of the conference and have specific questions in mind. Pre-plan with your contact on the other side, too. Last but not least, make sure that both classes bring a visual element to the process, whether it be posters, charts, pictures, a skit, etc. Since video conferencing is a visual medium, it makes sense to take advantage of it.

Video conferencing has outstanding applications in the classroom. Think of the power of showing your students what other cultures look, sound, and dress like, for example. Think of the personal connections your students can make to authors or experts in the field. Imagine the ways you can collaborate with others around the world on projects, ideas, or problems. The potential for authentic, powerful use in the classroom is limitless.

OTHER ISSUES TO CONSIDER

→ It's important to note that all video conferencing programs (MSN Messenger, Yahoo! Messenger, AOL Instant Messenger, Google Talk, etc.) function in much the same way as Skype: install the program, add contacts, start messaging/video chatting.

→ Video conferencing fits well with other tools in this resource, as already noted with Google Docs. You also could use ePals to connect with a class and then video conference to develop that connection even further!

→ When conducting sessions with people of different cultures, make sure to take into account language differences and accent issues. Even though both parties may be able to speak the same language, accents can sometimes slow communication. In cases like this, the chat feature of the program you are using will be very helpful–if the students cannot understand a particular question or comment, type it out.

→ Most video conferencing programs also have a screen-sharing feature. This means you can collaborate on a project on the same screen, at the same time, from anywhere in the world!

→ Make sure to connect via a stable, high-quality Internet connection. Instability or a slow connection can make video conferencing frustrating and counter-productive.

One day, one of my students asked me about the Welsh language. I knew almost nothing about it other than what it looked like, so I sent an email to Dave Stacey, a social studies teacher from Swansea, Wales. The culminating activity involved Dave Skype-ing into my classroom and having a Q&A with my students... Dave and I co-facilitated the session as I passed the microphone around the room like a talk show host, taking questions from my students for Dave to respond to in real time.

DAMIAN BARIEXCA
Former English Teacher

CONTENT AREA TIE-INS

Science

→ Plan collaborative experiments with two classes. Both classes conduct the experiment with the same set of directions (perhaps with the directions created together through a Google Doc). Students can then show the experiment live to the other class and speak about outcomes. Did both of the experiments achieve the same results? Why or why not?

→ Take the laptop (and webcam) outside to show the other class live video of the climate, weather, animals, and plants that live in the area.

→ Collaborate on a project to better the environment in each respective place. Projects can be outside (picking up garbage, recycling) or inside (making the classroom and school greener).

Math

→ Work with another class to collect and analyze data that helps illustrate differences in culture. Questions posed could be about the number of electrical outlets, TVs, books, family members living at home, etc. Create charts with the data to share.

→ Create a regularly scheduled "stump the students" problem-solving showcase. Each week, one class challenges the other by proposing a math problem. In the following session, the class with the problem shows how they worked together to craft a solution and then poses a problem back the other way.

→ Practice measurement concepts via video chat. One participant holds up an object and asks the other class to estimate its length, width, volume, etc. Measurements are then made and predictions revisited.

TOOL #26
VOICETHREAD

CONTENT AREA TIE-INS

Language Arts

→ Upload an excerpt from a book your students are reading. Pose specific questions and encourage conversations about each idea.

→ Have students upload their writing samples to VoiceThread for peer review and revision.

→ Upload a piece of poetry and encourage conversation about why the author chose certain words. Extend this idea by asking students to create and upload their own versions of the poem that uses synonyms for many of the words within the original poem.

Math

→ Analyze word problems and their key-words. Discuss what each keyword means within the problem and how that helps to reach a solution.

→ Upload an unfinished proof and encourage conversation about possible next steps.

→ Allow students an opportunity to keep an online math journal. Students upload problems they are having trouble with and talk through their ideas and frustrations. Teachers can then comment back upon each journal entry with hints and suggestions.

→ Have students "show their work" using VoiceThread. Upload a set of problems and ask students to log in and give comments. What's more, when commenting in a VoiceThread, students can draw out their solutions right within the thread.

GOAL: STUDENTS ENGAGE IN A GROUP CONVERSATION THAT INCORPORATES VOICE, PICTURES, DOCUMENTS, AND VIDEO.

OVERVIEW

VoiceThread allows users to engage in a virtual conversation using visuals, voice, and documents. This highly collaborative environment, located at www.voicethread.com, promotes focused discussions around images, video, or documents that are uploaded and commented upon by the VoiceThread's creator. Users can then log in and comment on the item in five ways: through text, with a microphone, over the telephone, via webcam video, or with an audio file.

BUT FIRST...

→ To record voice comments for use within VoiceThread, you will need a microphone attached to your computer. To record video comments, you will need a webcam. Newer computers are usually equipped with one or both of these devices.

GETTING STARTED

The process originates with the creation of a VoiceThread account. Once you are logged in, follow three steps to publish your own VoiceThread: Upload files, comment on each new page, and share your creation either publicly or privately. When ready to begin, just click "Create" at the top of the main page.

Once in the creation engine, you can choose from a multitude of file types to upload, including common image files (JPG, GIF, BMP, PNG), common video types, PowerPoints, PDF files, and Excel spreadsheets. Each is automatically separated into its own page (for example, a three-page PowerPoint slide would be separated into three separate pages within VoiceThread). Once pages have been uploaded, you can easily add titles to each.

The next step is to add comments to each page. Most VoiceThreads rely on comments delivered through a microphone attached to your computer (the "voice" in VoiceThread). However, you can also utilize a text comment or use a webcam video. Make sure that your voice or webcam comments are clear and loud enough to be heard easily without making major adjustments to computer or speaker volume.

Once the presentation is finished, you can publish and share your VoiceThread in a number of ways. You can choose to copy the link to your VoiceThread and simply send the link to whomever you would like to invite into the conversation. When doing this, you can allow the public to view and/or comment on your creation. If you would rather keep your VoiceThread private, you can choose to add individual e-mail accounts for sharing.

USE IN THE CLASSROOM

VoiceThread is a wonderfully easy-to-use tool that encourages collaboration both in and out of the classroom. It is all about cultivating ongoing, rich discussions on whatever you choose to upload. The process engages students, as it gives them the opportunity to directly comment upon a document anywhere they have an Internet connection. The process should go both ways; not only teachers can upload documents (and control the conversation), but students should create their own VoiceThreads for peer comments.

The variety of uploadable formats is a huge plus for classroom use. Conversations can center around images, voice, and text in many different forms. Students can comment about virtually anything that is written, depicted, or spoken–from a famous speech, an excerpt from a novel, a painting, a photograph, or a piece of student writing submitted for peer review.

OTHER ISSUES TO CONSIDER

→ One VoiceThread feature allows you to moderate and approve your students' comments before they are published. To do this, click the "Publishing Options" button at the bottom of the editing screen.

→ VoiceThread operates **www.ed.voicethread.com**, a domain that offers more benefits to teachers. The environment is accountable, meaning that every account is a known user and can therefore be traced. All content uploaded to this domain is created or vetted by members of the **www.ed.voicethread.com** community. The cost to enter into this community is listed on the VoiceThread website (as of this writing, a K-12 teacher can operate under this environment for a $10/month or $60/year fee).

→ When you use this tool with your students, make sure that you encourage them to speak clearly into their microphones. This might take some practice, but it helps to avoid a common problem on VoiceThread in which one comment is hard to hear and the next one is too loud. There's nothing worse than turning your volume all the way up to hear one comment and then being blasted by the next.

One of my favorite collaborative projects came in the form of a VoiceThread project with my kindergarten students in Germany. Through the project, we collaborated with young children in Turkey and New Zealand to create a dialogue about our favorite animals... The project helped my students learn about different cultures and about how different children around the world speak English.

SHELLY TERRELL
English

CONTENT AREA TIE-INS

Science

→ Have students upload a series of images that show the steps in an experiment and then comment on the process they went through and the conclusions they were able to take away.

→ Upload a science video and encourage discussion as to the questions it poses.

→ Find or create a spreadsheet of scientific data, such as rising global temperatures. Upload and encourage a conversation about the data results or predicting trends by using the data to justify each position.

Social Studies

→ Ask students to create an online biography of an important historical figure by uploading pictures and commenting on the significance of each to that person's life.

→ Upload a spreadsheet or graph that contains data about the country or region under study. Encourage discussion about the mean of the data and how it's changing over time.

→ Upload primary source documents and stimulate discussion as to what the pieces can tell us.

TOOL #27

WEBSITE CREATORS

CONTENT AREA TIE-INS

Language Arts

→ Have students create a page based on the novel they are reading. Pages can include the plot, setting, character descriptions, etc.

→ Create a vocabulary page that evolves as needed. Any time a word comes up that students are unfamiliar with, ask them to look it up and provide a definition. Post this definition to your vocabulary page and give credit to the student(s) who researched it.

→ Host students' stories so their friends and family can view them. You can add files to your site easily in Weebly, so why not post your students' stories to your page so parents and other relatives can see their work?

Math

→ Have students collaborate to create a website at the end of the year for the math students who will be in your class during the next school year. They can try to explain some of the concepts they found most difficult in kid-friendly terms and offer advice to rising students on how to be successful in your class.

→ Create a page for homework help. On this page, you can give help and hints as to how homework can be completed. If you're feeling adventurous, you can create a video using screen-recording software (found on p. 72 of this book), upload this video to YouTube, and embed the video into your site.

→ Have students come up with challenging word problems and post them to a page. Other students can check the page and attempt to solve the problems in class for extra credit.

GOAL: STUDENTS CREATE EASILY PUBLISHED INTERACTIVE WEBSITES.

OVERVIEW

Website creators allow users to quickly and easily create and publish professional-looking Web pages. Weebly (**www.weebly.com**) ranks among the best and easiest classroom tool I've found. Others to explore are listed in "Other Issues to Consider."

Weebly is packed with features and is completely free to use as of this writing. Building a truly interactive, professional website has never been easier. The editor itself is drag and drop and incorporates WYSIWYG (What You See Is What You Get). Hosting of the website is also provided free of charge. In other words, with Weebly anyone who can operate a mouse can easily create a website with a unique address, viewable by anyone with an Internet connection.

BUT FIRST...

→ If you are planning to add student accounts, any child below the age of thirteen must have written parental consent to participate.

→ Check with your IT department to see whether or not you are able to create a separate class page from the one the school has assigned to you. Also, check your school's acceptable use policies to make sure students are able to post pages (without identifying information, of course).

GETTING STARTED

Weebly is available for general use but also now offers a fantastic opportunity for educators at **www.education.weebly.com**. Register first and complete some basic information about your school.

Next, set up your class. You'll name the class, specify the grade level, and decide whether the students' Web pages will be public or private. If you choose private, you will then enter a password to protect the pages from the general public. Add student accounts next (you can add up to forty). You can do this by entering each student or by importing a spreadsheet file. Once your students are added, you can print the list and give each student his or her login information. With this information, students can log into **www. students.weebly.com** and get started editing their own password-protected websites.

Students will first name their sites. Because the Weebly editor itself uses drag and drop, it's simple to use and edit. You can choose where to start by selecting one of the tabs at the top of the editor: 1.) Elements: Add elements such as images, text, columns, or plug-ins such as YouTube videos or Google Maps. 2.) Design: Play with the design/theme of your site. 3.) Pages: Add pages for structure. 4.) Settings: Manage the setup options for your site.

It is important to remember the WYSIWYG editing style. Whatever the page looks like in the editor is what it will look like when you publish it to the Web, so there are no surprises when you hit the "Publish" button. Within the editor, you can drag objects to new places, add text by clicking inside text boxes, and delete elements.

The "Pages" tab allows you to create new pages that will be automatically linked to your homepage. Navigation is handled automatically as well. You will also see an option to add a blog page to your site. This is easy to create and equally as simple to post to.

Once you have your site looking the way you like, it is time to publish it to the Web. By clicking the "Publish" button on upper right-hand side, you get three choices: Option A allows you to freely host your site with Weebly, giving you an address that will look something like **www.testingthisout.weebly. com**. Option B allows you to pay for and register your own site name, which will drop the Weebly part off (for example, instead of **www.testingthisout. weebly.com**, you can purchase **www.testingthisout.com**). If you already own a domain name and want to transfer the Weebly page to this domain, choose Option C. For your purposes with students, Option A is most likely your choice; Once chosen, Weebly automatically posts and hosts it to the site name you chose. It is just that easy!

USE IN THE CLASSROOM

Posting a unique website as a class website/blog is, of course, an excellent instructional tool. But it can do so much more. For example, students can create their own Web presence, collaborate in groups to publish a site about any topic being studied, and use their site to interact with friends, families, and other students around the world.

Finally, digital portfolios are being utilized more and more (and rightfully so). Weebly offers an easy, free space for housing student digital portfolios, which I discuss in Chapter Four.

OTHER ISSUES TO CONSIDER

→ Other possible options for easy website building:

1. Google Sites (meshes well with other Google tools, such as Google Forms, Calendars, and Documents): **www.sites.google.com**
2. Wix (gives flashier design options than Weebly, but does not provide student accounts): **www.wix.com**
3. Webs (similar to Weebly, but no student accounts): **www.webs.com**

→ With Weebly, you can host up to forty student accounts for free under your account. More than this and you will have to upgrade to Weebly Pro.

→ You can upgrade to Weebly Pro with a varying monthly charge (depending on how long you sign you for). This gives you the ability to include 100 MB file uploads, an audio player, and ten sites.

→ Because Weebly has no calendar options, you cannot add a simple calendar to Weebly within the structure of the editor.

→ Weebly incorporates an easy way to sell products within the website editor. This can be useful for school organizations.

→ Remember that if your school blocks YouTube, you will not be able to view those embedded videos.

CONTENT AREA TIE-INS

Science

→ Create a page that classifies species, landforms, types of weather, planets, or any other topic you are working on. Each page will then contain pictures, information, and possibly video about each classification category.

→ Have students create a website from the point of view of something they are studying, such as bacteria or an endangered species (have fun with this!)

→ Have students create a website that they update daily about measurements taken in class each day, such as temperature, barometer readings, rainfall amounts, etc.

Social Studies

→ Have students create a government Web page about a country they are studying. Pages could include statistics about the country, information about the structure of its government, prominent leaders, currency, etc.

→ Utilize the Google Maps plug-in element to have students create a page about a particular place in the world. They provide the map, images, and information about what can be found there.

→ Ask students to create a website from the point of view of someone from a culture they are studying in class. Posts can consist of daily life, typical family structure, diet, etc.

TOOL #28
WIKIS

CONTENT AREA TIE-INS

Language Arts

→ Work on word usage to extend your in-class writing instruction. For example, you can put bland sentences onto the wiki such as, "Billy rode his bike into town to get something. What he saw on the way surprised him." Ask students to log into the wiki and revise the sentences so they are more descriptive and engaging.

→ Build a story on the wiki! Start off with a story-starting sentence and then ask students to go into the wiki and add whatever they want. Watch the story evolve outside of class, and discuss within class the twists, turns, problems, solutions, motivations, characters, setting descriptions, etc.

→ Use the wiki as a space for students to recommend books to their peers. Set up a short template for a book report, and ask students to add the books they read outside of class.

Math

→ Assign groups to different pages, each with a set of problems to solve. Groups work together to solve the problems and post solutions. Compare solutions and present ideas to the class. Tell other students they can visit the wiki outside of class and add to other groups' ideas and solutions.

→ Have students create their own wiki pages to display what they know about math topics currently being studied (For example, some students might create a page explaining how to find the area of a circle, etc.)

→ Invite students to a wiki page where they can critique the day's lesson, as well as whether or not the information should be presented in a different way.

GOAL: STUDENTS UTILIZE AN EASY-TO-EDIT WEBSITE FOR COLLABORATIVE ACTIVITIES.

OVERVIEW

What in the world is a wiki? Simply put, it is a website that users can log into and edit. The word itself is Hawaiian for "quick," and the first to apply it to this Internet function was Ward Cunningham. The success of Wikipedia (**www.wikipedia.org**) can certainly be cited as a major shift in how the World Wide Web is viewed and used by many users—away from its role as a broadcaster of information toward a platform where users actively participate with its content. No other tool exemplifies this movement like wikis.

BUT FIRST...

→ The main browsers for editing wikis are Internet Explorer, Firefox, or Safari. If you have problems editing a wiki, it is most likely due to the browser you are using. Try a different one to see if the issue resolves itself.

GETTING STARTED

With a wiki, the user is in charge. Content can be added and deleted, backgrounds and fonts altered, pictures added and removed; it is Web democracy at its purest. When you set up a wiki and invite students to participate, you are giving them the proverbial keys to the car. Not only giving them the keys, but also encouraging them to drive wherever they want, change the paint colors, and keep it for all hours of the day or night! Allowing students to work with wikis is a transformative teaching practice because you will be handing control to the students.

Two of the most popular and easiest-to-use wikis are PBworks (**www.pbworks.com**) and Wikispaces (**www.wikispaces.com**). Visit both sites to view examples before you make your choice. Once you have chosen a winner, it is time to register and set up your first wiki.

I highly recommend setting your first wiki up as a "test" wiki, one that you and only you will probably ever see. Here, you can practice adding pages, titles, working with a navigation bar, customizing colors and fonts, inserting pictures, etc. This practice will lead you to see how easy wikis are to use and edit.

Do some planning before your set up your first "real" wiki. What do you want to accomplish? Are you going to use the wiki for group work? If so, you will need to create group pages with instructions for each group on every page. Are you using the wiki to elicit responses to questions? If that's the case, you will need to give enough space so that students can respond in full. The number of pages you create and the titles and directions for each should be thought about carefully before you tackle your first useable wiki.

Once you have your wiki set up, it is time to start inviting others to view and/or edit. To do this, you will explore settings options. Here you will find the option to make your wiki viewable by all or just those who are invited. You can also specify if anyone with an account can edit the page, or only those who you invite. Those who you allow to edit will be able to edit anything within the site. Once you have accounts and permissions set up, you are good to go! Make sure to check **www.edtechsteve.com** for videos explaining these processes for both Wikispaces and PBworks.

USE IN THE CLASSROOM

Wikis are powerful tools simply because they transfer ownership to the student. Students get a lot of satisfaction from the inherent trust involved in opening up a wiki in this way. You can utilize this tool in all kinds of easy ways: put a question on a page and elicit responses, assign groups to work on a task online, brainstorm ideas, publish information, and on and on.

Another great aspect of wikis is that they are available to students wherever they have access to the Internet, at any time of the day or night. With the successful implementation of wikis in your classroom, don't be surprised to see your students logging in at night and over the weekends to offer more contributions or tweak previous ideas!

OTHER ISSUES TO CONSIDER

→ It's a good idea to back up the pages you are asking students to work on, especially if it's their first time on the wiki. You can do this by creating a Word document titled "Wiki Backup" and copying/pasting content there. If a student accidentally deletes a page or large chunks of work, you will be able to recover it easily.

→ Make sure to let students know they are being tracked. Both PBworks and Wikispaces attach a student's name and e-mail address to every edit.

→ Tell students not to delete, but to cross out ideas. If you are revising a sentence on the wiki, for example, students should not delete other students' ideas but cross them out so they can be recovered if needed. This also helps to validate all ideas presented.

→ When leaving comments, students should include their name on the wiki next to what they have added or changed. They can do this either by putting their name in parentheses or by signing their name to their changes with a dash in front. This allows easy tracking of who said what, without having to ask the students for this info or poring through the edit logs.

My law students created an online wiki to list and explain Pennsylvania's criminal laws in layman's terms. We partnered with a school in Tennessee, who created their list on our wiki. We also discussed the similarities and differences in the laws through the discussion feature. We will be completing this project again this semester and will be adding new states to join us in the comparisons.

DAYNA LAUR
Law & American Studies

CONTENT AREA TIE-INS

Science

→ Ask students to record their observations during experiments within the wiki. Color coordinate each sense they were using to make observations (red=sight, green=touch, blue=hearing, etc.)

→ Use wikis to record and publish data from surveys. Have students log into the wiki to give analysis of the data and draw conclusions. Other students can then log in and discuss by supporting or contradicting the conclusions given.

→ Utilize the wiki as an ongoing predictor of weather. Have students research the day's temperature, barometer reading, humidity, etc., and try to come up with a five-day forecast. Each day, assign a student or group of students to update the wiki with what actually happened the previous day. Leave space for students to come to the wiki and discuss why the predictions were on the mark or not.

Social Studies

→ Pose geography riddles on the wiki. Start a page and give some clues as to what area you are focusing on (clues could be statements, images, latitude/longitude coordinates, etc.) Ask students to log in and try to research/guess the area or landmark you are going for.

→ Create a page for each key vocabulary word and ask students to add images, video, audio, or quotes that represent the word in question.

→ Post a speech or an excerpt from a speech and ask students to go into the wiki and rewrite it in "today's" language.

WORD CLOUDS

CONTENT AREA TIE-INS

Language Arts

→ Create clouds from passages of different authors to reveal similarities and differences in tone and word usage.

→ Compare and contrast genres and how they emphasize different writing conventions, transitions, etc.

→ Copy and paste student writing samples into Wordle for collaborative or individual revision. All those tired, overused words will be visually redundant.

→ Copy and paste a week's worth of writing from the entire class into Wordle to create a composite view of word usage and variation. Do one at the beginning of the year and one at the end to see how these skills have progressed throughout their studies.

→ Make word clouds of the definitions of vocabulary words students are working on. Distribute and see if your class can identify the vocabulary word in question.

Math

→ Analyze word problems in a whole new way by copy/pasting a set of word problems into Wordle to analyze key words and clues for solving.

→ Have students write out the process they used to solve a problem. Next, ask them create clouds of their processes and compare them with other class members.

→ Have students enter a data set to create a cloud. Use this to talk about frequency and teach different ways of representing data. By default, Wordle strips numbers from the word cloud, so click the "Language" menu and uncheck "Remove Numbers."

GOAL: TO ANALYZE WORD USE THROUGH CREATION OF A PICTURE.

OVERVIEW

Word clouds are visual representations of text. They create cloud-shaped pictures based on the frequency of words used in a passage. The more often a word is used, the larger it appears in the cloud. This tool was first popularized by the photo-sharing site Flickr (**www.flickr.com**), which now uses it to visually display the most popular picture descriptions (or "tags") being uploaded to their site. The practice of word clouds is now widespread across the Internet.

BUT FIRST...

→ Wordle requires Java, so be sure to have the latest version installed. You can download the latest version at **www.java.com/download**.

GETTING STARTED

By far, the most popular tool for building word clouds resides at Wordle (**www.wordle.net**). Once arriving at this site, simply click on the "Create" button to get started. This takes you to a page where you can paste text into a text box or enter a URL to analyze a website or blog's word usage. Simply click "Submit" to create the word cloud.

Once the cloud has been created, it can be fully customized. Fonts, colors, shapes, and layouts can all be altered (there is also a "Randomize" button below the cloud that will automatically pick settings among all of these to create your cloud). Buttons below the cloud allow the user to directly print their creation or save to the public gallery stored at **www.wordle.net/gallery**.

One drawback associated with this process is that there is no easy, one-click way to take this image and convert it into a picture file for use in other applications. The print-screen function located on every standard Windows PC keyboard allows you to convert the image for other uses. Hitting this key takes a picture of whatever is on your screen and copies this picture to the clipboard.

The next step is to paste this picture into another program. You can paste it directly into any Microsoft program (Word, PowerPoint, Excel) or photo-editing software (Adobe Photoshop, Microsoft Paint). From there, you will need to crop the picture to focus in on the word cloud itself. On a Mac, this process is much easier: just utilize the shift-command-4 combination to select the word cloud and it will save to your desktop; or, use the Grab application to take a screenshot.

USE IN THE CLASSROOM

Word clouds provide powerful classroom opportunities to think critically about text. The ability to analyze passages in a straightforward visual format can really help connect your students to text. Students can compare/contrast speeches, articles, or author passages. They can analyze their own or their peers' writing in class. Students can analyze websites to determine underlying tones or messages that may not be blatantly obvious. There aren't many limits to the uses of word clouds to analyze text.

OTHER ISSUES TO CONSIDER

→ Wordle is an unfiltered website. While the front page will not show any profane word clouds, the gallery will. Direct your IT department to unblock **www.wordle.net** and instead block **www.wordle.net/gallery**, **www.wordle.net/next**, and **www.wordle.net/random**. This will block the offending links but still allow you to utilize Wordle with students.

→ It is possible to link phrases together in Wordle by joining the words or phrases with a tilde symbol: ~ . For example, by entering "twenty~first ~century~learning," the word cloud will illustrate the phrase as "twenty first century learning" when generated.

→ WordItOut (**www.worditout.com**) is another word cloud choice.

→ Images created in Wordle are licensed under a creative commons attributions license. This means that they are available to use in whatever venture you desire, as long as the image is attributed to **www. wordle.net**.

My fifth and sixth graders used the tool to give a quick snapshot of what they learned about Internet safety from a video we watched. I could tell from the words they chose whether they had completed watching the video and whether they took away the vocabulary and concepts I wanted them to.

MARY BETH HERTZ
Computers

Science

→ Have students copy and paste observations they have made while watching or performing an experiment. Compare clouds to reveal the different words students use to describe the same experiment.

→ Use a descriptive paragraph to create a cloud about a certain planet in our solar system. Show the cloud to students and see if they can determine which planet it is describing (this would be a good activity for any kind of categorization—landforms, types of rocks, types of animals, parts of a cell, parts of the body, etc.)

→ Have students keep a log of food intake for the week to show what foods they are eating most often.

Social Studies

→ Compare and contrast speeches by historical figures to determine word choice. Have students think critically about what this means regarding the speaker's intent, current situation, audience, and persuasive abilities.

→ Paste URLs of various news sites to analyze reporting bias. Analyze the the stories that are getting the most attention on different news sites.

→ Copy and paste a list of objects, customs, unique holidays, or other information associated with a particular country. Students try to identify the country and explain their answers (and say whether or not anything else could have been added for further clues).

TOOL #30

ZOHO

Language Arts

→ Allow students to take notes as a group using Zoho Notebook and the sharing/collaboration features within.

→ Upload a Zoho Writer document with several pages, each with a picture/name of a different character from the novel you are reading. Ask students to log into this document and list the physical and emotional attributes of each character.

→ Create a Zoho Writer document with a table of the five senses. As a title, use a setting such as the beach or the school cafeteria. Have students log into the page to provide detailed descriptions of things they might experience with their senses in each setting. Talk about why this is important when developing a story.

Math

→ Group students up to collaborate on a spreadsheet where each member of the group is required to find certain information/numbers and make calculations. For example, a group of three students could work on a spreadsheet about the nine tallest buildings in the world. Each member is responsible for finding a third of the buildings (along with their height, date constructed, etc.) then performing calculations (such as average height, years since built, etc.)

→ Upload a "Problem of the Week" and invite students to access it and attempt to solve it collaboratively.

GOAL: TO UTILIZE A WIDE ARRAY OF ONLINE TOOLS TO CREATE, SHARE AND COLLABORATE.

OVERVIEW

Zoho (**www.zoho.com**) offers itself as a one-stop source for free online productivity applications. Whether you need a word processor, spreadsheet, database, presentation, document manager, organizer, notebook, wiki, project planner, or e-mail application, Zoho has it. As of this writing, all were offered without charge. All of the applications "talk" with one another, which allows for easy collaboration.

The applications also handle file types supported by Microsoft Office applications, such as MS Word, Excel, Access, or PowerPoint, so each of these file types can be easily loaded into Zoho. Each application is housed in the cloud, so you can retrieve and work on your documents anywhere you have an Internet connection without the need to buy or download software. Finally, each application allows collaboration, meaning you can invite and share documents among peers. The nice part about Zoho is that it combines many of the tools in this book into one place—collaborating on documents, creating chat rooms, web conferencing, wikis, and more.

BUT FIRST...

→ Zoho relies on Java and Flash, so make sure both of these are updated before you start.

GETTING STARTED

Registration at **www.zoho.com** is the first step. Once you've registered and logged in, you will be confronted with the full array of applications to choose from. This list can be overwhelming, but this is a good thing because it means you have a lot of tools to choose from and explore.

A good, comfortable place to start is by exploring the Zoho versions of spreadsheet, presentation, and word processing applications. These are titled Zoho Sheet, Zoho Show, and Zoho Writer. You can find them listed under "Productivity Apps" at the top of the page. Enter each of these tools and get a feel for how they look and function. Any document that you upload or create can be saved to Zoho by clicking the save button. Documents can also be saved as different file types (including PDFs) to enhance translation and the ability to move between applications.

After experiencing the tools that you are most likely comfortable with, it's time to start exploring other Zoho tools like the Zoho Planner, which helps you keep a to-do list and calendar. Zoho Notebook allows you to take notes online that can incorporate images, text, video, audio, or HTML. These applications and others offer a lot of opportunity for trial and error. The true power of Zoho lies in its ability to combine many tools in one spot, from wikis to chat rooms to collaborative documents.

USE IN THE CLASSROOM

Zoho represents another strong set of integrated tools that function in the cloud. For this reason alone, it is a powerful tool to share with your students.

OTHER ISSUES TO CONSIDER

→ Zoho is a good, free solution for students that may not have MS Office at home.

→ Users can only collaborate on a document if they are registered Zoho members. The document can be viewed by non-Zoho members, but cannot be edited. This is a significant drawback, as it means that everyone who edits a document must already be registered as a Zoho user (which can slow things down).

→ There is a 1 GB space limit for Zoho Docs.

→ Collaboration is in real-time. In other words, two or more people can work on the document at the same time —when one changes something, it updates the document for all that are working on it.

→ There is plenty of debate about whether students "need" to learn how to use Microsoft Office, or if they should simply learn the broader skills of working with productivity software (word processing, spreadsheet, presentation software, etc.) Since there is no way to predict exactly what software your students will be using in their future schooling, careers, or home life, it makes more sense to show them a variety.

→ OpenOffice, another free program suite that simulates/replaces MS Office, is available for download at OpenOffice.org (**www.openoffice. org**). This is a good solution for students who cannot afford MS Office for their home computers.

CONTENT AREA TIE-INS

Science

→ Have students utilize Zoho Planner to post projects with reminders and lists of the tasks they need to accomplish to finish on time.

→ Contact a local official that is in charge of water purification and share a list of student ideas about the process by using Zoho Writer or Zoho Show. Invite the official into the document to clear up misconceptions and steer students toward a better understanding of the process water goes through to become safe and drinkable.

→ Have students conduct experiments at home and create a Zoho Show presentation to share their processes and what they learned (the amount of guidance you do or do not give for this experiment is up to you).

Social Studies

→ Create blank country fact sheets and have students log into each to research and enter missing information.

→ Partner up with other classrooms around the world and share a presentation between the classes that outlines important cultural differences and similarities.

APPENDIX

EVEN MORE E-TOOLS!

The following is a list of excellent digital tools with many classroom applications. They didn't make the cut because they were too content-specific, expensive, or were more oriented toward teacher use. However, these highly recommended tools still merit exploration.

Tool	Description
ASLPro.com **www.aslpro.com**	The ASLPro.com American Sign Language dictionary provides a great opportunity to link vocabulary with sign language. The site contains short clips of actors who demonstrate how to do the signs for words within the ASL dictionary. This is a great resource for kinesthetic learners!
Delicious **www.delicious.com**	Delicious is social bookmarking, which means that users can upload their favorite links to their Delicious account and then share these links with the world. Bookmarks and lists can be tagged so that other users can quickly find relevant links.
Digital Booktalk **www.digitalbooktalk.com**	Digital Booktalk showcases books in the form of video "trailers," much like those shown in movie theaters or online. The short book trailers introduce the basic plotlines and attempt to "hook" the viewer into reading the books. Students can also create and submit their own trailers.
Diigo **www.diigo.com**	With the Diigo service, users can not only save and share bookmarks, but can also annotate Web pages. Groups can be created to collaborate on the same Web page (which can be archived, so that if the page disappears you still have access to it.) Diigo also offers premium educator accounts that allow you to create and manage student users.
Edmodo **www.edmodo.com**	Edmodo is similar to a Ning in that it allows you to set up a class site to share assignments, links, documents, polls, and calendars with your students. Think of it as a repository for class work and a place for students and teachers to interact in a secure, online manner.

Flickr www.flickr.com	Flickr is a photo-sharing website that allows you to upload and tag photos that can be easily searched by the public. One powerful aspect of Flickr is that it maintains a common catalogue of images. Some users upload the pictures to Flickr and allow the public to incorporate them into their own work, as long as the photographer is attributed. If there is an photo you would like to use, look for the "Request to license" link near the license on the photo page. If you don't see it, you can contact the member directly for permission.
Geocaching www.geocaching.com	Geocaching is "a high-tech treasure hunting game played throughout the world by adventure seekers equipped with GPS devices," as described on the site, **www.geocaching.com**. The basic idea is to take students out into nature to locate a hidden box using a GPS device and the provided location. Once found, you sign the logbook inside of the box. Inside the cache can also be any number of items: puzzle clues, problems to solve, pieces of a plot, etc. If you remove something from the cache, you are supposed to leave something of equal or greater value. This is an excellent way to get students who love nature involved in your classroom, as well as a fun, kinesthetic way to build knowledge.
Google Wave www.wave.google.com	As of this writing, Google Wave is still in the experimental stages. It looks to be a new way of collaboratively communicating by combining aspects of e-mail, chat, video chat, document sharing, and wiki principles. A user starts a "wave" that other participants can ride too, posting and replying to one another in real time. The conversation can be saved, and users will be able to insert pictures, audio, video, and links. This one is definitely worth checking on as time goes by.
Moodle www.moodle.com	Moodle is a course management system. It can deliver courses online through an extensive feature set that includes the ability to post announcements, assignments, manage discussion boards, blogs, documents, and many other useful tools. If you are interested in pursuing Moodle within your school or school district, you will need to contact your IT department, as it needs to run from a local server.

Morse Code Translator http://morsecode.scphil-lips.com/jtranslator.html	When students enter text, this JavaScript Morse code translator converts the message to dashes and dots, which can then be played over computer speakers. The translator works both ways, too. Kids love to create and pass codes to one another, and this is a fantastic way for your logical/mathematical students to work on language.
OpenOffice www.openoffice.org	OpenOffice is a free alternative to Microsoft Office. It is open source, which means that many programmers work together to eliminate kinks in the program. They then open this process up for all to see and collaborate on. This is a great alternative to suggest to students who may not have MS Office on their home computers but still want the same functionality. It comes packaged with five core products: Writer (word processing), Calc (spreadsheet), Impress (presentation), Draw (drawing/image manipulation, and Base (database).
Posterous www.posterous.com	Posterous is one of the easiest ways to start blogging or journaling online. There is no sign up necessary—all you need is an e-mail address. Just send an e-mail to post@ posterous.com. The subject line becomes the title of your blog post, the body is the text, and any images, videos, links, MP3s or other files you attach to the e-mail are automatically added. After you send the e-mail, Posterous will reply back to you with a link to your new blog post! With the rise of smart phones and other Internet-ready devices such as the iPod touch and iPad, this type of service can be an easy way to post ideas and communicate with the world.
Story Bird www.storybird.com	Story Bird allows students to easily create stories for online publication. Students first choose art provided by professional illustrators, then add their own text. With an account, they can invite others to collaborate on the story and publish it as well. Anyone with an Internet connection can see the story after it is published. This is an *excellent* online story creator that is intuitive and very easy to use.

VoxSwap **www.voxswap.com**	VoxSwap bills itself as the "social network for learning languages." It allows users to upload instructional videos of themselves teaching their native languages. Users can "friend" each other to help this language acquisition process along. The site is growing every day and appears worthwhile, especially for foreign language teachers.
Wallwisher **www.wallwisher.com**	On this simple site, users can create a virtual wall to post text, images, video, or links. As of this writing, the site does not require registration for either the originator or the visitors. This means that a wall can be set up and activated in less than a minute. The announcement wall resides in the clouds and can be assessed and used by parents, students, and colleagues wherever there is an Internet connection. Users simply go to the URL (which the host determines), double click, and add information. It's a very quick and simple way to create an interactive space online.
World of Warcraft **www.worldofwarcraft.com**	A video game in education? Absolutely! World of Warcraft is just one example of a game that can be used effectively in the classroom. Many games involve a high amount of strategy, collaboration, and problem-solving. Many higher-order thinking processes can be targeted through gaming, all while reaching out to students in the worlds they live in when they get home from school. Many virtual gaming worlds have rich history, character development, and important choices embedded directly into the fabric of the environment. I urge you to consider gaming as a part of your classroom! (For information on how World of Warcraft is being successfully integrated into schools, visit **www.wowinschool.pbworks.com**).
xtranormal **www.xtranormal.com**	Xtranormal is a fun way to create animated movies online. You choose the scene and the actors, type in their parts, animate them, and let them interact, bringing all kinds of content to life. Students can enter any text, and the characters will speak the dialogue. You can also record audio for use with the animated characters and put an extra, personal touch to the action. The movies you create in xtranormal can then be shared publicly through e-mail, Facebook, MySpace, or as a published link.

To find more tools and resources and to get updates on the tools in this book, be sure to visit my website at **www.edtechsteve.com**.

THE INTERNATIONAL SOCIETY FOR TECHNOLOGY IN EDUCATION (ISTE) NATIONAL EDUCATIONAL TECHNOLOGY STANDARDS (NETS-S)

21ST CENTURY TOOL	Creativity and Innovation	Communication and Collaboration	Research and Information Fluency	Critical Thinking, Problem Solving, and Decision Making	Digital Citizenship	Technology Operations and Concepts
Animoto	✓				✓	
Blogs		✓			✓	
Collaborative Whiteboards		✓		✓		
Digital Storytelling	✓				✓	
ePals		✓			✓	
Glogster	✓	✓				✓
Google Docs		✓				✓
Google Earth	✓		✓			
Google Forms			✓	✓		
Image Editing	✓					✓
Live Internet Video Streaming		✓				
Message Boards		✓		✓		
Mind Mapping	✓	✓				
Ning		✓		✓		
Podcasting		✓				✓
Prezi	✓					✓
SchoolTube	✓	✓		✓		
Screen Recording		✓		✓		
Second Life	✓	✓				
SlideShare		✓	✓			
Spore Creature Creator	✓					✓

Timeline Creators	✓		✓			
TodaysMeet		✓			✓	
Twitter		✓	✓			
Video Conferencing		✓		✓		
VoiceThread		✓				
Website Creators	✓	✓		✓		
Wikis		✓				✓
Word Clouds	✓			✓		
Zoho		✓		✓		✓

PERFORMANCE INDICATORS FOR STUDENTS

1. **Creativity and Innovation**
   Students demonstrate creative thinking, construct knowledge, and develop innovative products and processes using technology.

   Students:

   → a. apply existing knowledge to generate new ideas, products, or processes. (*Mind mapping, timeline creators, website creators, word clouds*)

   → b. create original works as a means of personal or group expression. (*Animoto, Digital storytelling, Glogster, image editing and enhancement, Prezi, SchoolTube, Spore Creature Creator, website creators*)

   → c. use models and simulations to explore complex systems and issues. (*Google Earth, mind mapping, Second Life, Spore Creature Creator*)

   → d. identify trends and forecast possibilities. (*Timeline creators*)

2. **Communication and Collaboration**
   Students use digital media and environments to communicate and work collaboratively, including at a distance, to support individual learning and contribute to the learning of others.

   Students:

   → a. interact, collaborate, and publish with peers, experts, or others employing a variety of digital environments and media. (*Glogster Google Docs, podcasting, SchoolTube, SlideShare, TodaysMeet, video conferencing, VoiceThread, wikis*)

   → b. communicate information and ideas effectively to multiple audiences using a variety of media and formats. (*Blogs, collaborative whiteboards, ePals, live video Internet streaming, message boards, mind mapping, Ning, SchoolTube, screen recording, Second Life, TodaysMeet, Twitter, VoiceThread, website creators*)

   → c. develop cultural understanding and global awareness by engaging with learners of other cultures. (*Live video Internet streaming, video conferencing*)

   → d. contribute to project teams to produce original works or solve problems. (*Collaborative whiteboards, Google Docs, message boards, Ning, SchoolTube, video conferencing, wikis, Zoho*)

3. **Research and Information Fluency**
   Students apply digital tools to gather, evaluate, and use information.

   Students:

   → a. plan strategies to guide inquiry.

   → b. locate, organize, analyze, evaluate, synthesize, and ethically use information from a variety of sources and media. (*Google Earth, Google Forms, message boards, timeline creators*)

   → c. evaluate and select information sources and digital tools based on the appropriateness to specific tasks. (*SlideShare, Twitter*)

   → d. process data and report results. (*Google Forms*)

4. **Critical Thinking, Problem Solving, and Decision Making**
   Students use critical thinking skills to plan and conduct research, manage projects, solve problems, and make informed decisions using appropriate digital tools and resources.

   Students:

   → a. identify and define authentic problems and significant questions for investigation. (*Google Forms*)

   → b. plan and manage activities to develop a solution or complete a project. (*Collaborative whiteboards, Ning, SchoolTube, screen recording, Zoho*)

   → c. collect and analyze data to identify solutions and/or make informed decisions. (*Google Forms, VoiceThread, word clouds*)

   → d. use multiple processes and diverse perspectives to explore alternative solutions. (*video conferencing, Zoho*)

5. **Digital Citizenship**
   Students understand human, cultural, and societal issues related to technology and practice legal and ethical behavior.

   Students:

   → a. advocate and practice safe, legal, and responsible use of information and technology. (*Animoto, digital storytelling, TodaysMeet*)

→ b. exhibit a positive attitude toward using technology that supports collaboration, learning, and productivity. (*ePals, TodaysMeet*)

→ c. demonstrate personal responsibility for lifelong learning. (*Blogs*)

→ d. exhibit leadership for digital citizenship.

6. **Technology Operations and Concepts**
   Students demonstrate a sound understanding of technology concepts, systems, and operations.

   Students:

   → a. understand and use technology systems. (*Podcasting*)

   → b. select and use applications effectively and productively. (*Glogster, Google Docs, image editing and enhancement, Prezi, wikis, Zoho*)

   → c. troubleshoot systems and applications.

   → d. transfer current knowledge to learning of new technologies. (*Spore Creature Creator*)

TEACHER CASE STUDIES

ANIMOTO:

Christina DiMicelli
Hampstead Academy
Hampstead, NH
Subject(s) taught: Computers/Technology
Grade level(s) using tool: 5th, 7th, 8th

We joined an online wiki collaboration for six-word memoirs. I had grades 5, 7, and 8 use worksheets and online refrigerator magnets to create their own six-word memoirs. Once they had their words, they went online and searched for images. They needed to find two images for each word, and the visual representations that students used for words was very interesting (someone used chain links to visualize "and"). Using Animoto, students took their twelve images and added their six words. After choosing music, their videos were created. We uploaded them to the collaboration wiki after having class viewings. The students liked the idea that their designs are exhibited for a global audience. The grade 5 class hopes to connect with another school in the project for extension activities, such as a discussion on why they chose their words. The wiki is here: **www.6wordmemoir.wikispaces.com/Hampstead+Academy**

BLOGS:

Alfonso Gonzalez
Chimacum Middle School
Chimacum
Subject(s) taught: Science
Grade level(s) using tool: 6th, 7th, 8th

My science students follow up class projects and labs by blogging about their experiences at **www.mrgonzalez.org**. I post assignments in the form of follow-up questions or ask students to share their conclusions. Students are able to add Glogs to their blog and sometimes we make video podcasts or commercials to post on the blog. Students can do their blogging at home, at lunch, or after school. I also give class time to blog and communicate with our blog pal classrooms…When students are working on their blogs, I rarely have to help them and don't find myself having to ask students to get on task. The room feels high-energy with the buzz of science and tech talk.

Jennifer Duarte
Mountain Vista
Colorado Springs
Subject(s) taught: 6-8 ELL (English Language Learners)
Grade level(s) using tool: 6th, 7th, 8th

This is the first year that I have used blogs with my middle school students. I started with a Ning network last year, but really wanted to take my students out into the real world. We have just started writing our first official blog. Their engagement level is amazing. They are struggling to discover a topic that they are passionate about and that their readers will also be passionate about. They fret over word choice, factual information, and the structure of the document. It has taken their writing to a whole new level. They really enjoy the personalization of their blog and the fact that they have their own Web address. We talk about their digital footprint and this is a great way for them to begin developing a positive footprint—one that they can be proud of.

COLLABORATIVE WHITEBOARDS:

Sherry
Bethel Elementary
Midland
Subject(s) taught: N/A
Grade level(s) using tool: K, 1st, 4th, 5th

FlockDraw was an effective learning tool when used with fourth and fifth graders to help review technology vocabulary words. Groups of students were assigned to draw a picture of a word, label it, and type a brief description of how it was used. As with any cooperative learning group exercise, roles had been established. Some groups chose to have an artist and two writers. Other groups allowed group members to choose words they would most like to illustrate and describe individually. Flockdraw turned a dull vocabulary lesson into a creative, collaborative masterpiece. I used Flockdraw with kindergarteners and first graders to review 2D and 3D shapes. The students worked in pairs, drawing the different shapes and labeling them. This activity developed higher-level thinking skills as partners collaborated to determine which shapes to draw, who would draw them, and which tools were necessary in order to complete the task. The students were anxious to share their work with classmates via the interactive whiteboard.

DIGITAL STORYTELLING:

Gayle Cole
The Center for Early Education
Los Angeles
Subject(s) taught: Tech Integrator
Grade level(s) using tool: 4th

A fourth grade teacher at the Center for Early Education (where I work) gave an optional assignment for students to share something about their free reading book. She gave them choices of ways that they could do their "book report." As one option, students could work with me, the school's instructional technology facilitator, to make a "book trailer"—a book review resembling a movie trailer. Two girls chose this option. I worked with the them using Microsoft Photo Story to create their "trailer" about the book *The Music of the Dolphins*. At the time, we had not used Photo Story before, so all three of us found it very exciting to explore together. I had the students begin by creating a storyboard. Once they had carefully planned what to include, we talked about how to gather the images they would need. The process was smooth and simple, but they had such strong opinions and creativity that we found we needed additional time outside of their class period. The girls eagerly agreed to meet with me during their lunch and recess times! Once we had inserted the images, they worked on text. We worked hard to keep things clear, concise, and easy to read. Finally, we worked on sound. The girls were perfectionists, enjoying their craft to the point I imagined them working for a major movie studio in the future. After the girls created their "book trailer," they showed it to the rest of the class using the SMART Board. Everyone loved it! I immediately had requests from more students to help them learn to use Photo Story as well. The teacher was so pleased, she put the project on her class Web page for a month. Other students decided to check out the book from the library.

EPALS:

Mirjana
Speak Up English Language School
Kragujevac
Subject(s) taught: English language
Grade level(s) using tool: 6th, 7th, 8th, 9th, 10th

We've been using ePals for seven years. The inital idea was to connect our students with some students from another country. We were really surprised by the number of schools interested in collaborative projects. The first project we did was the "Cinderella Project" with a school from Great Britain. They were supposed to compare different versions of the story. My students were thrilled. Apart from helping them make new friendships, they learned how to write an e-mail—it improved their writing and reading skills, as well as gave them an opportunity to learn something about another culture. Also through ePals, we made a contact with a school from Topeka, Kansas, and our 13-to-17-year-olds had a Skype meeting with their peers. That experience also helped them improve their communication. Also, we initiated a project called "Around the Globe," where schools from around the world sent us their PowerPoint presentations or videos about their schools, communities, and way of life. We also exchange some podcasts with some schools in the USA.…We reached a much higher goal then just meeting new people and improving our English.

Irem Ebru Gursoy
Umitkoy Anatolian High School
Ankara, Turkey
Subject(s) taught: English
Grade level(s) using tool: 9th

I have been using ePals to have my students communicate with other classrooms around the world to practice their English and also learn about other cultures. I also use this tool to find teachers who would like to collaborate with me on a project. The students like the English language a lot when they use this tool. They understand that it is more than a subject at school. They force themselves to develop their English skills in a very secure environment. Also, they are more motivated when I teach in the classroom. They are more excited about learning English, and they are more careful when they are writing and speaking English.…Also, the partner teacher who I found through ePals and I organize student exchanges. We host them in our country and they host us in their country, which is a great experience in our students' lives.

Pat
Notre Dame Academy Elementary
Los Angeles
Subject(s) taught: All
Grade level(s) using tool: K

I used ePals last year and this year with my kindergarten students. All of our experiences have helped my students gain an appreciation for different cultures and the significance of written communication. We used every opportunity to learn about the world and geography. Students also recognized the importance of serving others and protecting our environment. Last year, we corresponded with pen pals in Spain and Italy. We exchanged Flat Stanleys and conducted an evaluation of the nutrition habits of our classes. This year, we participated in the project "I've Got No Strings'" with our pen pals in India. Our classes chose a folk tale from our countries, made puppets, performed and recorded the puppet show, and exchanged with our new friends. This year, my class entered and won the Countdown to Copenhagen Students Speak! Contest on the ePal's website. Our PowerPoint, *Hands Across the World*, was on the DVD presented to the world leaders and scientists at the Copenhagen Climate Conference in December 2009.

GLOGSTER:

Bernard Waugh
Kannapolis Middle School
Kannapolis
Subject(s) taught: Social Studies
Grade level(s) using tool: 7th

We have used Glogster several ways in my class; however, I believe the most impacting project we did centered around a research project. I had my students pick a human rights violation from the area of Africa or Asia, then research details about it. Instead of having them do a paper on it, I asked them to do a Glog. We had some lessons on what would make an effective Glog, but I really just asked them to have fun, be informative, and push the limits a little bit. The projects I got back were powerful, and the students were impacted. I witnessed student researching harder than they had previously. They were gathering forms of data they had not before, like videos and photographs. I had encouraged them to keep the writing to a minimum, so I saw them sorting through information for the best stuff to put in their Glogs. Overall, I witnessed the students approach this project as true students—curious, intelligent, and excited. They were using high-level skills that I could not get out of them in a traditional paper format.

GOOGLE DOCS:

Jennifer Duarte
Mountain Vista
Colorado Springs
Subject(s) taught: ELL (English Language Learners)
Grade level(s) using tool: 6th, 7th, 8th

I have used Google Docs in various ways this year. When we create a rubric, I create the document on Google and then share it with my students. This way, they constantly have access to the expectations of the project. I have also used Google Docs when my students are writing their Amazon book reviews. They create their draft in Google Docs, they share it with me, I provide feedback, and then they make the changes needed. Since they don't have to continually rewrite the paper, the edits are of a higher quality. Moreover, it is easier for me to work paperless than carrying around reams of papers to grade. When they are ready to post their review on Amazon, all they have to do is copy and paste. Not only are they creating writing that they are passionate about, but they are using real-world skills to do it.

GOOGLE EARTH:

Karen Mann
A T Allen
Concord, NC
Subject(s) taught: All core classes
Grade level(s) using tool: 5th

The fifth grade science unit on landforms includes a section on "bird's eye view" and "side view". The students were given an area on campus to make a scaled model with interlocking blocks placed on a mock terrain in a rectangular pan. Then a transparency with a printed grid was taped on top while the students drew the bird's eye view. We realized that the students didn't really understand the abstractness of this activity, so we changed the lesson. Now we begin by taking the students to Google Earth and looking at the area around our school. Then we visit a variety of other places the students would recognize before turning them loose to do their own "world traveling." After discussing what we saw on Google Earth and how it compares to what we see here on the ground (side view), we begin the science lesson on bird's eye view. Students now have a better understanding of bird's eye view and are able to apply it to the small mapping skill described above.

GOOGLE FORMS:

Michael Kaechele
Valleywood Middle School
Hudsonville
Subject(s) taught: Technology, Math
Grade level(s) using tool: 6th, 7th, 8th

I use Google Forms in two ways. First, I use it to make my class paperless. Students take their notes in Google Docs and then submit them to me weekly in a simple Google Form. I like this system because it is efficient, paperless, and gives me all of the student answers in one, neat spot. Students like it because they do not lose their papers—a major problem for many middle school students! I also give pre-tests to my sixth grade math class before each unit. The pre-tests are around ten questions, but give me a quick way to evaluate my students' skill level on the new topic. I like the graphs that I can create from the results to summarize the strengths and weaknesses of their existing knowledge.

Ann Gregson
Northwest Cabarrus High School
Concord, NC
Subject(s) taught: Math (PreCalculus & Algebra II)
Grade level(s) using tool: 9th, 10th, 11th, 12th

I have used Google Docs and Google Forms as a means of assessing students. I have used the Google Docs feature as a way to insert images and equations into my test for more versatility in question types, and then use a Google Form to collect the answers. Having the students input answers into a Google Form allows the answers to go straight into a spreadsheet for easy grading. If the teacher takes the test first, then the first row of the spreadsheet is an automatic key! I use the cell fill features to marks answers right and wrong. The different types of questions on a Google Form allow for multiple choice, short answer, and ratings, which offers an even more versatile test.

Matt Harriger
Mooresville Intermediate School
Mooresville, North Carolina
Subject(s) taught: Reading
Grade level(s) using tool: 6th

I was looking for a way to make sure my students were reading every day without having to do a "Reading Log." I didn't want to go through the hassle of making sure parents signed the reading log with no way of knowing if the students actually read. I started giving the students the first fifteen minutes of class as silent reading time. Every time the kids finished a book, they were to go to the Google Doc where they could answer questions about the book. It worked great! I had them reading, I could check their understanding, and I didn't need to get parents to sign anything.

MESSAGE BOARDS:

Greg Garner
Moore MST Magnet School
Kilgore, TX
Subject(s) taught: Technology Applications
Grade level(s) using tool: 8th

This is not breaking news to most middle school teachers, but students are very social. Edmodo provides a way for my students to interact with each other, learn about each other, and communicate—all in a private, controlled environment. Students who would never raise their hand in class will lead discussions online and Edmodo has provided the ability for me to incorporate online, outside-of-class learning with "traditional" classroom instruction. I was hesitant about bringing in such a powerful tool as only a second-year teacher, but the same day I showed my students this website, I logged on that evening to find four of my students quizzing each other (in real-time) about an upcoming history quiz, using the threaded discussion feature as a way to track their responses, and referring back to tougher questions. Six months later, I cannot imagine teaching my class without Edmodo!

MIND MAPPING:

Meredith Stewart
Cary Academy
Cary, NC
Subject(s) taught: Language Arts and Social Studies
Grade level(s) using tool: 6th

As part of our study of the Japanese samurai and their code of honor (bushido), students used SpicyNodes, a mind-mapping website, to create a map of their own virtues. They selected virtues they imagined would be useful for them in their lives from a list of classical virtues and then answered a series of questions, selecting one virtue per question. After students had finished their writing, they created a node map, with each virtue represented as a node. The definition of the virtue and the student's answer to the questions he or she had selected for each virtue was a sub-node. SpicyNodes allowed students to customize the way their writing was presented, and this resulted in a creation that was easily embeddable in each student's blog.

NING:

Hadley Ferguson
Springside School
Philadelphia, PA
Subject(s) taught: History
Grade level(s) using tool: 8th

The assignment was for students to write letters to their US senators on an issue that interested them. I created a Ning with discussions for the major issues that were discussed on the websites of the two senators. The students went to the websites and posted what they learned about the issues that they were interested in. They read each other's posts and added to them, creating a rich collaborative environment. They each then chose an issue that they wanted to write about, having read all of the information that the group had gathered. They wrote their letters and posted them on their page of the Ning. Then I assigned two or three letters for each student to read and edit. After the letters were edited, they were rewritten and then sent to the senator by e-mail and by snail mail to track response time.

PODCASTING:

Dodie Ainslie
Vestal Central Schools
Endicott, NY
Subject(s) taught: Reading
Grade level(s) using tool: 6th

My students created podcast interviews with characters from the books that they read. Once they finished reading the book, they would pick a character and write the interview questions and answers. The answers had to be "in character," and they could choose to do both voices (interviewer and character) or have another student assist them with the recording. We used Audacity to record and edit, then we published online. The students loved doing these first podcasts so much that they started their own team: "6CNN News Cast." These episodes were produced weekly and included interviews, homework/studying tips, "fun happenings," announcements, and other special news about our team and school. The students even had a contest for our opening and closing music, which ended up being written and recorded by one of our students. The biggest impact that I saw? Students really become more of a community around the news podcast. Anytime we incorporated podcasts, students were more motivated to do their best and be creative. I got such great, creative projects—much more than I ever got with any "traditional" book project. They also listened to each other's projects more and were more inclined to read books that were recommended to them.

PREZI:

Ann Gregson
Northwest Cabarrus High School
Concord, NC
Subject(s) taught: PreCalculus, Algebra II
Grade level(s) using tool: 9th, 10th, 11th, 12th

The first time I used Prezi in the classroom to present a lesson, the kids' eyes went bug eyed! They had never seen anything like it. The swooshes and zooms and fonts were totally new and engaging. I was quite shocked to see that a new tool (I had been previously using PowerPoint) would grasp their attention so differently. They were instantly interested in the information and the delivery tool. Prezi also makes a math person smile because of its non-linearity. It helps the teacher and student see a much larger picture. It's not one after another— it's a huge sheet of paper with lots of information that we can jump around on.

SCREEN RECORDING:

Michael Kaechele
Valleywood Middle School
Hudsonville
Subject(s) taught: Technology, Math
Grade level(s) using tool: 6th, 7th, 8th

I love using screencasting tools with my students to publish my students' work on their blogs and on our class wiki. My students program games in Scratch, make 3D drawings in Google SketchUp, and stop motion animation videos in Pivot Stickfigure Animator (for examples: **www.chacoo.edublogs.org**). Then students use Screentoaster or Screencast-O-Matic to record their projects. Screencasting is simple to do, but powerful because the tools create an embed code; students can easily share their projects with the world.

SECOND LIFE:

Julie LaChance
Northwest Cabarrus High School

Concord
Subject(s) taught: Technology
Grade level(s) using tool: 12th

I first used Second Life with a group of Computer Applications 2 students because a new part of their curriculum is the use of virtual worlds. Not too long after that, however, a student from that class came to me for help using Second Life in his graduation project. I have been mentoring this student through the process of building a multi-level greenhouse in the virtual world. In addition to the build, he has also been speaking at conferences, both face-to-face and virtually, and talking with educators from all over the world that have stopped in to look at his project. This project has become a learning process that spans many curriculums, and it has built his presentation skills and communication abilities—as well as challenged him to think more creatively.

SPORE CREATURE CREATOR:

Jennifer Yandle
J.N. Fries Middle School
Concord, NC
Subject(s) taught: Exploring Biotechnology
Grade level(s) using tool: 7th, 8th

While teaching the genetics unit to my exploring biotechnology class, I thought it would be fun and interesting to incorporate the Spore technology into the lesson. To set up the project, each trait (phenotype) within the Spore program was assigned a genotype. To begin the project, students were given a worksheet with the designated genotypes for the male and female creatures and the Punnett squares needed to create the offspring. I designated genotypes for both a male and female Spore creature and the students were responsible for the rest of the project. The first part of the project was students creating their male and female Spore creatures based on the provided genotypes. Next, students complete Punnett squares for each trait to determine the possible genotypic and phenotypic possibilities of their offspring. Students chose what they want their offspring to be, based on the possibilities they came up with. To wrap up the project, students create a document including the pictures of their created Spore creatures, genotypes used, and a paragraph describing the phenotypic traits displayed by their creatures. If students finish the project early, the next part of the assignment was to write a fictional story about their Spore offspring. I encourage the students to add animations of their creatures and include them in their story presentation. This activity allowed students to explore their creative side while practicing the fundamentals of genetics.

TIMELINE CREATOR:

Steven Anderson
Clemmons Middle School
Winston-Salem NC
Subject(s) taught: Instructional Technologist
Grade level(s) using tool: 6th, 7th, 8th, 9th, 10th, 11th, 12th

In my class, students have made timelines on various topics. In some cases, they were organizing all of the major battles during World War II or describing the events surrounding the Civil Rights movement. Other times, they were creating a timeline of the major events in their lives. Before they had access to the Web, students would purchase poster board, brightly colored paper, and markers to create timelines. Timelines created in Timetoast not only look good, but they also have features that make them useful for learning. For example, students can enter images and text about an event on the timeline and add links to more information about the event or cite resources. One of the best examples I have seen of students using Timetoast is in a middle-school history class. Students had been investigating the travels of various explorers and world travelers. (Lewis and Clark, Christopher Columbus, Magellan, etc.) The students conducted research and created lists of Web resources. For example, they referred to diaries that these explorers maintained through their travels. Using the diaries, students were able to create dynamic timelines that included images, quotes, and links that described the journeys of their traveler.

VIDEO CONFERENCING:

Damian Bariexca
North Hunterdon High School
Annandale, NJ
Subject(s) taught: School psychologist, former English teacher
Grade level(s) using tool: 11th, 12th

When I was an English teacher, I taught an Honors British Lit class. Part of that class covered the history of the English language—its development from Old English to Middle English to Modern English. One day, one of my students asked me about the Welsh language. I knew almost nothing about it other than what it looked like, so I sent an email to Dave Stacey, a social studies teacher from Swansea, Wales, with whom I've corresponded on Twitter. Over the next few weeks, Dave, my students, and I collaborated on an ad hoc mini research project about Wales, fueled primarily by my students' curiosity. We set up a wiki page where my students archived the questions they had for Dave, and Dave visited the wiki to provide some basic answers and provoke further questions.

He also prepared a handout on Wales for my students. The culminating activity involved Dave Skype-ing into my classroom and having a Q&A with my students. I had a ceiling-mounted LCD projector connected to my tablet PC, which I used to project Dave onto a screen. His voice came through wall-mounted speakers connected to my tablet. Using some masking tape and pushpins, I attached a webcam to a cork strip over my whiteboard and pointed at the center of my classroom. My class of about eighteen students scrunched together in the middle of the room so Dave could see them all, and Dave and I co-facilitated the session as I passed the microphone around the room like a talk show host, taking questions from my students for Dave to respond to in real time.

VOICETHREAD:

Shelly Terrell
Deutsch-Amerikanische Zentrum
Germany
Subject(s) taught: English
Grade level(s) using tool: K, 1st

One of my favorite collaborative projects came in the form of a VoiceThread project with my kindergarten students in Germany. Through the project, we collaborated with young children in Turkey and New Zealand to create a dialogue about our favorite animals. The idea was to find a way to encourage my German-speaking students to use the English they learned. I had the children do drawings of their favorite animals. Their parents were assigned the task of having the children practice the English at home. The kindergartners from Turkey contributed a story about animals, while the children in New Zealand spoke about their favorite animals. The project helped my students learn about different cultures and about how different children around the world speak English. This is very important at a time when cultural stereotypes exist in our area. I am hoping that these connections will inspire children to extinguish these stereotypes and to learn to speak English.

WEBSITE CREATORS:

Christina DiMicelli
Hampstead Academy
Hampstead, NH
Subject(s) taught: Computers/Technology
Grade level(s) using tool: 6th

After talking about digital footprints and Internet privacy, each sixth grader created their own Weebly site. They designed and added avatars and personalized their sites. In conjunction with a language arts project, students did research on ancient Egypt. Instead of making a tri-fold display or written research paper, they displayed their work on the Weebly sites. Working with guidelines and rubrics, each student researched information, found images, and created pages on their sites to display their work. We covered digital citizenship, information literacy, creativity, innovation, communication, etc. The students were thrilled with this new medium for expression, especially the ability to personalize it. Being a Web 2.0 tool, students had easy access to their work at home. Parents were impressed with the products as well. Many of the students have taken the time to extend their Weebly sites with researched topics of personal interest.

WIKIS:

Dayna Laur
Central York High School
Harrisburg, PA
Subject(s) taught: Law, American Studies, AP US Government
Grade level(s) using tool: 11th, 12th

My law students created an online wiki to list and explain Pennsylvania's criminal laws in layman's terms. We partnered with a school in Tennessee, who created their list on our wiki. We also discussed the similarities and differences in the laws through the discussion feature. We will be completing this project again this semester and will be adding new states to join us in the comparisons.

WORD CLOUDS:

Mary Beth Hertz
Bluford Elementary
Philadelphia, PA
Subject(s) taught: Computers
Grade level(s) using tool: 1st, 5th, 6th

With my first graders, I let them type in any words they knew how to spell. Or, they could create a Wordle to tell about themselves, typing their name a few times so it was big and adding words about their interests or their family. This project accomplished a few goals. First, I wanted a fun way to give my little ones practice finding letters on the keyboard. I also wanted to give them a chance to practice spelling words they knew, while also challenging them to add new words. My fifth and sixth graders used the tool to give a quick snapshot of what they learned about Internet safety from a video we watched. I could tell from the words they chose whether they had completed watching the video and whether they took away the vocabulary and concepts I wanted them to.

Ann Leaness
MLK High School
Philadelphia, PA
Subject(s) taught: English
Grade level(s) using tool: 11th

I copied and pasted part of Benjamin Franklin's autobiography into a Wordle and gave it to my students as a pre-reading assignment. They had to guess the topic we would be reading, the main idea, and some details we would be reading about. They really liked it, and were able to tell me more than I thought they would.

Ben Knaus
Cityview Performing Arts School
Minneapolis, Minnesota
Subject(s) taught: AVID
Grade level(s) using tool: 6th, 7th, 8th

I've used [Wordle] to reflect on speakers. During a speech, I have students take notes, trying to fill in an A-Z list with key words. Then, I take the notes and put them into a Wordle. The result is a stunning reflection on what the speaker was all about. I've done this twice—once with a Peace Corps volunteer and once with an army sergeant.

GLOSSARY OF DIGITAL TERMS

Avatar: A virtual or digital representation of one's self. Often referred to with computer games, your avatar is the character you create to represent yourself within the game environment.

Backchannel: This refers to a conversation that occurs beneath the layer of the central conversation or topic at hand. For example, if a presentation is being made, a back-channel chat room can be used for listeners to make comments or suggestions without disrupting the presentation at hand.

Cloud Computing: Also known as "the cloud," this refers to the Internet. Cloud computing therefore refers to storing documents, applications, and ideas on the Internet rather than the traditional storage space—on the hard drive of your personal computer. Items stored "in the cloud" are therefore accessible from anywhere you have an Internet connection.

Digital Footprint: An individual's digital footprint refers to the trails he or she leaves behind (both wanted and unwanted) on the Internet. These trails can come from message board posts, e-mails, social networking sites, blogs, picture sites, or anywhere else on the Internet.

Digital Portfolio: A collection of digital products selected by students to show their mastery of content and growth as a learner.

Embedding: This refers to taking an online product and placing it within a website of your choosing. This is done through an "embed code"– a series of letters that you copy and paste into the site you are using to display work. A good example of this is when you allow your students to create digital portfolio websites. If they create a digital timeline, they can copy the embed code from the timeline creator and paste it into their digital portfolio website. The timeline will then show up directly on the site, without forcing the user to follow a link to view it.

E-tool: Short for electronic tool, this is any tool used electronically. Most of these are now housed on the Internet.

Hashtag: A word or phrase with a pound (#) symbol in front of it. Hashtags are used in Twitter to group conversations or ideas together so that users can track comments easily (for example, ideas about education reform use the tag #edreform). Twitter users can then search for conversations based on hashtags. Hashtags are also often used at conferences to help the participants conduct group conversations in real time about the happenings at the event.

PLN (personal learning network or professional learning network): A PLN is an individual's network of resources that he or she relies on to grow as an educator. The tools are dependent on the user but often include blog subscriptions, Twitter, Ning, message boards, or RSS feeds. The purpose of the PLN is to learn as a community and continuously think and improve upon your practice.

RSS Feed: Commonly known as "Really Simple Syndication," an RSS feed comes from websites that often update their content. These could be blog posts, YouTube video channels, news sites, etc. These sites put out an RSS feed, which is then subscribed to by a user. The user then sets up a "feed reader" (such as Google Reader) to compile the updated information into one spot. In short, RSS feeds allow you to have the information you want come to you, stored in one easy location, instead of you needing to incessantly check all your favorite sites to see if they've been updated.

Tags: These are words or phrases that you attach to items you upload to the Internet so that the items are easier for others to find when searching. For example, when uploading a video to YouTube about cats, you would include "cats" in the tag section of the video upload screen. Then, if someone is searching for the term "cats" on YouTube, your video would come up in his or her search results.

Tweeps: This is the Twitter version of the popular slang, "peeps," as in "my people."

Twenty-First Century Classroom: A learning environment that allows students to utilize technology to collaborate locally and globally, create products, and publish these products to the Internet.

Twenty-First Century Learner: A learner who collaborates locally and globally, creates products, and publishes his or her products to the Internet.

Twenty-First Century Teacher: A teacher who allows his or her students opportunities to collaborate locally and globally, create products, and publish these products to the Internet.

Twenty-First Century Tool: Any type of technology that allows the user to do one or more of the following: collaborate locally and globally, create a product, and/or publish a product to the Internet.

Web 1.0: This describes the first generation of the Internet. This generation centered around people creating websites for others to read. Web 1.0 was static–you went to the Internet, searched for content, and then read websites about content. It was a top-down approach–webmaster posts content, user receives content.

Web 2.0: This describes the second generation of the Internet. This generation is characterized not by users simply receiving content, but instead creating their own content and publishing it to the Web. This content includes blogs, message boards, video uploads, audio file sharing, and much more. Web 2.0 is bottom-up–the users generate the content instead of simply receiving. It is interactive, rather than static.

WYSIWYG: Pronounced "Whizz-e-wig," this stands for "What You See Is What You Get." This refers to what you will experience when editing an online document. Most of this online editing is now WYSIWYG; in other words, the way you format the document is exactly the way it will show up to others when published to the Internet.

BIBLIOGRAPHY

Anderson, L. W., and Krathwohl, D. R. (Eds.), *A taxonomy for learning, teaching and assessing: A revision of Bloom's Taxonomy of educational objectives*. (New York: Longman, 2001).

Fisch, K. *"Did You Know?"* 2007. http://thefischbowl.blogspot.com/2006/08/did-you-know.html

Friedman, T. L.*The world is flat: A brief history of the twenty-first century*. (New York: Farrar, Straus and Giroux, 2005).

Gerstner, J. *"Don Tapscott: Digital dad- interview."* BNet, 1999. http://findarticles.com/p/articles/mi_m4422/is_1_17/ai_59228568/?tag=content;col1

Hertz, M. B. *"Why everyone needs a great PLN,"* http://philly-teacher.blogspot.com. (accessed September 9, 2009).

Tapscott, D. *Grown up digital: How the net generation is changing the world*. (New York: McGraw-Hill, 2009).

Wotham, J. *"More employers use social networks to check out applicants."* New York Times, 2009. http://bits.blogs.nytimes.com/2009/08/20/more-employers-use-social-networks-to-check-out-applicants

AUTHOR BIOGRAPHY

Steve Johnson started his career as a kindergarten and second-grade teacher in the rural town of Vass, North Carolina. Technology was always a big part of his classroom environment, and after six years he shifted over to a technology facilitator position. He has been a technology facilitator for five years, working with students and teachers in grades K-8 to enhance learning with technology tools.

Steve started writing when fate brought him and fellow Maupin House author Carol Baldwin together at a workshop where she presented on writing children's books. They worked together on the second edition of her book, *Teaching the Story*, which includes technology connections to the creative writing process. Steve's depth and breadth of experience with relevant technology tools, along with his experience as a classroom teacher, allows him to support teachers in their efforts to improve and enhance instruction.

Steve currently resides in Concord, North Carolina, with his wife, Bridget, and two little girls, Emily and Kenna.

NOTES

NOTES